Punishment and Political Order

Law, Meaning, and Violence

The scope of Law, Meaning, and Violence is defined by the wide-ranging scholarly debates signaled by each of the words in the title. Those debates have taken place among and between lawyers, anthropologists, political theorists, sociologists, and historians, as well as literary and cultural critics. This series is intended to recognize the importance of such ongoing conversations about law, meaning, and violence as well as to encourage and further them.

Series Editors: Martha Minow, Harvard Law School
Austin Sarat, Amherst College

Punishment and Political Order

KEALLY MCBRIDE

THE UNIVERSITY OF MICHIGAN PRESS
Ann Arbor

10733000

Copyright © by the University of Michigan 2007
All rights reserved
Published in the United States of America by
The University of Michigan Press
Manufactured in the United States of America
♾ Printed on acid-free paper

2010   2009   2008   2007   4   3   2   1

A CIP catalog record for this book is available from the British Library.

Library of Congress Cataloging-in-Publication Data

McBride, Keally D.
    Punishment and political order / Keally McBride.
        p.   cm. — (Law, meaning, and violence)
    Includes bibliographical reference and index.
        ISBN-13: 978-0-472-09982-5 (cloth : alk. paper)
    ISBN-10: 0-472-09982-5 (cloth : alk. paper)
    ISBN-13: 978-0-472-06982-8 (pbk. : alk. paper)
    ISBN-10: 0-472-06982-9 (pbk. : alk. paper)
        1. Punishment—Philosophy.   2. Punishment—Government policy.
3. Social control.   4. Sovereignty.   5. Punishment—Government
policy—United States.   I. Title.

HV7419.M398   2007
364.601—dc22   2006029795

To John

Contents

Acknowledgments

This project began while I was working with Mary Katzenstein at Cornell University on a John S. McKnight Postdoctoral Fellowship and I became interested in the phenomenon of prison labor. It developed even more at a National Endowment for the Humanities Summer Institute at Amherst College, led by Austin Sarat in the summer of 2002. He was most enthusiastic when I developed the idea for this book, and Jim Reische at the University of Michigan Press also carried me along through the writing process, encouraging me to write plainly whenever possible, having faith that a book can be both smart and pleasurable to read—even one on punishment. The other participants in the punishment seminar were stellar colleagues in every sense of the word, and I would like to thank Valerie Karno, Robert Gordon, Karl Shoemaker, Ted Sasoon, Alysa Rosenthal, Bill Lyons, and Christopher Sturr in particular for helping me begin to think about punishment and political theory and to write the first section of this book. I would also like to thank *Law, Politics, and Society* for permission to reprint "Hitched to the Post" here, and the reviewers who helped me to develop that argument.

John Zarobell, Kevin Bundy, Carl Cheeseman, Marie Gottschalk, Nancy Hirschmann, Betsy and Richard McBride, and the anonymous reviewers for the University of Michigan Press read parts of the manuscript and gave me excellent advice and conversation. Marie Gottschalk, *The Prison and the Gallows,* and Bruce Western, *Punishment and Inequality,* shared copies of their manuscripts (which have now been released), making it possible for me to benefit from their illuminating work on the American penal system today. Ruth Ost let me teach a seminar on punishment in the Temple University Honors Program, giving me a captive audience that helped immeasurably. My seminars on punishment at the University of Pennsylvania were also lively, helping me to reconceptualize the manuscript significantly.

My reading group—Jeremy Elkins, Steve Salkever, and Christina Beltran—helped me to tackle sovereignty, and Roger Berkowitz staged a well-timed intervention in my thoughts on the subject as well. Andrew Norris assisted my thinking about political order. Rogers Smith welcomed me at the University of Pennsylvania into the intellectual life of a wonderful department and provided the structural support to finish the project, while Valerie Ross encouraged me to think about academic writing very differently.

Though the professional support was crucial for this project, the personal encouragement was tremendous. Telling people that you are writing a book on punishment seems to bring out the nascent comedian in many folks. This good cheer helped counterbalance the at times weighty content of the project, and I am grateful for the love and support provided by my friends and neighbors: Katy, David, Michael, Karen, Steve, Sheila, David, Christine, Meg, Ken, Jane, David, Ben, Carola, Sandra, Gerry, Anne, Casey, Andrea, Mamatha, and Marvin. You picked up my spirits and children, gave me dinner and drinks, and without all of you I couldn't have survived my years dwelling upon punishment. Celeste and Theo asked more questions about it than I really wanted to answer, and they continue to demonstrate that you are never too young to be a philosopher or question the inherent justice of a punishment decreed. John, as always, maintained the quintessential balance between interest in my project and encouragement to think about something else, and he gave me support during my trials and provided the pushes needed to overcome them.

Introduction

Strange Brew—Punishment and Political Ideals

Though I didn't know it yet, I started writing this book when I moved to Philadelphia, into an apartment that was two blocks away from what appeared to be a medieval castle. The stone walls are dizzyingly high—three or four stories at least—and the front gate, complete with menacing spikes, is flanked by little breaks in the fortress walls that appear to allow shots to be fired from within. The building was Eastern State Penitentiary, the first full-fledged penitentiary in the United States and the object of study by foreign visitors such as Alexis de Tocqueville and Charles Dickens. It was one of the largest and most expensive buildings built in the United States at the time of its completion in 1829, and it takes up eleven acres in the midst of what soon became a lively urban neighborhood. The stone walls are so thick that the expense of tearing it down was enough to deter even the most avid redevelopers.

Today, community groups help provide attractive landscaping around the building, farmer's markets are held in the parking lot, and I even buy my Christmas tree there every year. The colossus is integrated into everyday life. I am reminded of the building's strangeness only by visitors who are both awestruck and confused by the incomprehensible architecture. Were there medieval settlements—in Philadelphia? The expanse of stone was designed to intimidate, and it still succeeds in the task. Yet the fortress has become a familiar part of the landscape, and even its neighbors overlook the intrusive aspect of it. The building personifies state punishment, though in a different way than was intended. The initial recognition may be shocking—remember the first time you understood that some people are put in jail, forever—but then we become accustomed to it. That is, we forget about the awesome power until we are forced to confront it through a shocking revelation, its direct intrusion in our lives, or the perspective of outsiders. As someone engaged in the study of politics, it is my central task to help bring a new awareness to these aspects of the political landscape that we take as settled or no longer even notice.

A few months after I moved to Philadelphia, I was asked to help organize a group that would think about how to decrease recidivism in those coming out of Philadelphia's current prison system. It was a task force on "reentry" and "reintegration"—was there any way to bring this population out of exile and back into the community? Ex-prisoners, parole officers, victims' rights groups, prison administrators, district attorneys, and criminologists sat around a table and talked once a month. There was a fundamental inability to decide on the basic story. Prisoners' rights advocates saw reintegration as contingent upon everyone understanding their punishment, their incarceration, as unjust. They could look around them and see that the prisons were full of minority males with little economic opportunity. Their incarceration was a reflection of social injustice as much as their individual crime. Why should they want to reintegrate into a political system that victimizes them and violates its own tenets of equality and justice?

The other group, the majority of those sitting around the table, assumed that the ex-offenders had something to prove to everyone else. They needed to amend for their crimes and prove that they had been rehabilitated by their incarceration. They needed to demonstrate a moral conversion before everyone would feel safe welcoming them back into the community. Not surprisingly, a standoff ensued. It was unclear who the victims were, who needed to make amends, and who was culpable. One of the curious dynamics of this group was that those who had experienced incarceration firsthand lacked general credibility. Punishment seems a particularly difficult subject to broach politically because those who are subject to it have no legitimate voice in any public debate in regard to it; and the rest of us take it for granted that it works just fine, particularly since it doesn't influence our daily lives. It is the colossus that we have become accustomed to. For others, however, it becomes the catalyst for radicalization, and the point where the ideals of a polity are most evidently betrayed.

I had been accustomed to think of punishment as an expression of force, a way of tracing the administration of power. Consider the common etymology of the words *execute* and *executive*; the ability to punish displays where the power of command rests. Michel Foucault's *Discipline and Punish* laid bare the history of punishment to demonstrate the shift in the constitution and exercise of political power; and though his argument is that political power is decentralized, he examines punishment largely as displaying executive capacity. We can be certain that the power to punish expresses ultimate authority and that those who are punished have less power than those who administer it.

Most of the current literature on punishment reflects this basic understanding. Punishment is seen as both an expression of and a tool for consolidating power, and also reflects historical and current racial and socioeconomic inequalities. This straightforward view of the relationship between power and punishment was challenged by my experiences teaching standard courses in the history of political thought. In the midst of utopian treatises, discussions of justice, and debates about the troubling division between thought and action I kept stumbling into yet another discussion of punishment. Why was this brutal, unpleasant intruder lurking in utopian visions and idealistic political constructions?

This book began as the answer to that question, and it contains many discussions about the role that punishment plays in various works of political theory. But like all works of political theory, this one is also concerned with the world outside of its pages. The primary purpose of this text is to look at punishment as a central problem of political order. Sociologists, legal scholars, and criminologists study penal regimes: the discipline of political science, with notable exceptions, has ceded this ground.[1] This is a terrible mistake: as I will demonstrate, punishment is both a uniquely revealing lens into how political regimes work as well as a central problem for political administration that requires careful negotiation of the stated ideals of a polity in the exercise of power.

One of the most consistently complex problems facing political theorists is understanding where power comes from. We have rightfully become increasingly dissatisfied with visions that focus only upon the state or even its figureheads. Yet understanding how behavior, law, institutions, perception, and ideals all work together in creating a political system is difficult to conceptualize. Examining punishment allows us to see the intersection of all of these different elements.

More than that, punishment allows us to see political order in dynamic fashion. To claim that consent, perception, display, and recognition play a role in the maintenance of political order is to say that relationships form the basis of political order. Relationships may sound like a static element, but they change repeatedly: consent isn't established just once, and perceptions aren't cemented in a moment of time; instead they change, break down, are reaffirmed or altered. How is it that regimes lose legitimacy even if their institutions remain in place? How is our support of a political order brought into question? These questions are just as important as examining how the status quo is maintained. Perception as a component of political order is difficult to account for on its own—like studying how a mirror distorts objects without being able to study the reflected object. Examining punishment allows us to understand how the perception of the public itself confers political legitimacy and sovereignty; only a legitimate entity can punish, all others abuse.

My other point, that punishment is a problem for political regimes, relates to this first one. Unjust punishments have served as a catalyst for uprisings at more than one point in recent history, and it is no accident that prisoners often become martyrs and then leaders as in the cases of Václav Havel and Nelson Mandela. For a state to punish does not seem remarkable—after all, it has that power. For a state to punish over a long period of time and not generate resistance to that expression of its power is a much more difficult, and rare, feat. It can only do so through a complex negotiation of idealism and force, which is why punishment, even though it is a universal attribute of regimes, is simultaneously one of their most difficult tasks. This fraught relationship between idealism and pragmatism in state punishment requires a more extensive introduction.

Political Idealism and Punishment

Most famously, both Aristotle and John Locke maintained that political order is distinct from other kinds of human collectivities. What separates the polis from other kinds of associations is a matter of considerable contention, but for the purpose of this argument I agree that it is distinct. The polis is marked by a juxtaposition of idealistic or normative elements with the problems of administration. It is impossible to find a regime entirely without norms, though it is all too easy to see regimes that fail to act according to these stated norms. Conversely, governmental administration could never be driven by ideals to the exclusion of practical considerations. Hence, one aspect of political order is the need to relate political ideals to the administration of a population.

State punishment exclusively reveals this interaction between ideal and pragmatic in political orders. First, it is the gap between normative and material that causes punishment. Punishment is administered only when an ideal fails to be realized, whether that is obedience to the king, laws, or social norms. State punishment is an attempt to reconcile disorderly realities or citizens with the ideal order. Though punishment rarely, if ever, produces ideal behavior or citizens, punishing those behaviors that fall outside of the norm reaffirms the state's commitment to that ideal. The effects of punishment are certainly embedded in the bodies and spirits of those subjected to it, but the rationale behind the practice displays an allegiance with an ethereal vision.

Second, punishment invites examination of whether the exercise of state power is actually bounded by its declared ideals. Weber's famous dictum that the state is defined by a monopoly of legitimate violence is important here.[2] The state is allowed a unique prerogative to capture, hold, even kill or maim its citizens. What makes such essentially brutal acts *legitimate?* The answer to this question is different in every regime; however, all states punish in the name of an ideal. Practices of punishment that continually contradict the stated ideals of a regime can ultimately lead to political destabilization. This is not an empirical study of exactly when such a tipping point occurs; however, one of my tasks is to reveal the fraught relationship between ideals and the administration of painful sanctions as one of the most difficult and central aspects of political order.

The claim that punishment is related to the idealistic claims of a political order should invite skepticism. After all, today punishment appears most frequently to be a violation of ideals of justice. To someone who is alarmed by the new severity in the penal code and administration of criminality in the United States, this sounds like an especially dubious theme to propose at this particular juncture. In the United States in the past twenty months we have debated whether it is right to execute persons who committed crimes when they were juveniles or mentally impaired, we have looked at pictures of prisoners being sexually molested, abused, and even killed by U.S. military police, and we have discovered secret prisons around the world intended to make our enemies disappear forever. While it may be an expression of the sheer power of the United States to engage in these activities, it is difficult to envision them as a reflection of our political ideals.

When a state punishes, its ideals are on display and at stake. To think of punishment as an ugly necessity that has no relation to the more lofty aspirations of justice leads to an ever more egregious and potentially destabilizing exercise of the state's prerogative to administer pain to those subject to it.[3] Just as a state should enter warfare and condone the sacrifice of its soldiers with trepidation, a state also needs to pay meticulous attention to its practices of punishment or risk its authority. Recently, the understanding of how integrally related punishment is to the stated ideals of a polity has been lost. We may not realize or understand that punishment is an expression of our ideals, but it nonetheless remains such.

As this seems a particularly untimely argument to make, a brief examination of past understandings of the relationship of punishment and justice is in order. The Greek words *timē* (honor) and *poinē* (punish) come from the same Indo-European root.[4] Implicit in the Greek understanding of both of these words is a reciprocal relationship, that every action demands a reply, a belief evident in Aristotle. An unjust action violates the proportional; therefore punishment is required in order to reassert the proportionality of justice. "As the unjust in this sense is inequality, the judge tries to restore the equilibrium. When one man has killed and the other been killed, the doing and the suffering are unevenly divided; by inflicting a loss on the offender, the judge tries to take away his gain and restore the equilibrium." It is crucial that the loss of proportionality not be perpetuated by the punishment; there is not a simplistic reversal whereby the judge subverts the offender as he or she had subverted the sufferer. "The only difference the law considers is that brought about by the damage: it treats the parties as equals."[5] State punishment cannot create victims.

Punishment is the infliction of pain. But for Aristotle, it is also the assertion of goodness. Because it is necessary in response to an infraction, and because it is done with the intention of reasserting balance, it is the source of goodness. It is preferable for a society never to punish, and a state that punishes without absolute necessity is no longer just. The measure of a just punishment is that it reestablishes proportionality in response to a crime. Even if the punishment itself is an equivalent action, such as capital punishment in the case of murder, if it is done out of necessity and in the interests of equality, it meets the standards of the good.

Hegel also elaborated a theory of punishment along these lines, through the distinction between revenge and punishment. Revenge is the natural right of the injured to inflict pain upon the perpetrator. In

Hegelian terms, the right of revenge is pursued out of a position of particularity; it has a personal dimension, which then reasserts the rights of the particular person who has been wronged at the expense of the universal. When punishment is levied in court, however, particularity of revenge is replaced by the universality of injured right.

> Instead of the injured party, the injured universal now comes on the scene, and this has its proper actuality in the court of law. It takes over the pursuit and avenging of crime, and this pursuit consequently ceases to be the subjective and contingent retribution of revenge and is transformed into the genuine reconciliation of right with itself . . . by the annulment of the crime, the law is restored, and its authority is thereby actualized.[6]

The reassertion of the power of universality over the particularity of injury or crime establishes the rule of law again. By punishing infractions in the name of its universality rather than in the name of a specific victim, the law is able to reassert its own dominance and the value of the universal over the particular, again and again.[7] The necessity of punishment may seem to indicate a lapse in the power of the law, but in the act of punishing, the law is reaffirmed. It is crucial to understand that the power of the law is not reaffirmed through its ability to expel members from the social body, or inflict pain, but rather because the values of universality and right are upheld in the process of punishment.

Hegel is clear that the assertion of the law through punishment is not achieved at the expense of the criminal who is punished. The prosecuted do not lose their rights or membership in the state through their punishment. Instead, Hegel argues that the punishment itself is a reflection of the criminal's rights, and ultimately an embodiment of his will. Only a free, rational person can undergo punishment. Through punishment, the state reaffirms that the criminal is a responsible agent.

> The injury which falls on the criminal is not merely *implicitly* just— as just, it is *eo ipso* his implicit will, an embodiment of his freedom, his right; on the contrary, it is also a right *established* within the criminal himself, i.e. in his objectively embodied will, in his action. The reason for this is that his action is the action of a rational being and this implies that it is something universal and that by doing it the

criminal has laid down a law which he has explicitly recognized in his action and under which in consequence he should be brought as his right.[8]

It is the criminal's right to be punished since rights derive from our existence as universal beings. Hegel also explicitly links the pain of punishment with the reassertion of justice. He argues that the person being punished has endured a sort of psychic split. As part of the universal, in repudiating the universal by breaking the law, she has rejected a part of herself. Philippe Nonet has explored Hegel's argument and asserts that the pain of punishment heals the split within the offender. Pain literally brings the offender back to the truth of universalism.[9] Hence, it is the relationship to the universality of the state and the law that creates punishment: all other retributive pain that derives from a particular relationship or injury is revenge.

What both Aristotle's and Hegel's descriptions of punishment have in common is that punishment is the reluctant office of the law and state. The state serves as the instrument of legality here; it cannot punish with the intent of enforcing or asserting its own power. Only if it meets the criteria of necessity and judiciousness can the state punish with impunity. Punishment then emerges as one of the crucial ways to measure the rule of law. How we punish reveals whether a society adheres to the rule of law. It is not the punishment itself that reasserts the rule of law, but rather the process used to determine whether a punishment is needed and what it shall be.

This notion that punishment needs to be dispassionate in order to be just is reflected in U.S. jurisprudence. For instance, in *Coppedge v. United States* the Court observed, "The methods we employ in the enforcement of our criminal law have aptly been called the measures by which the quality of our civilization may be judged."[10] Recognizing that the impulse for revenge may be strong, the law must stand in opposition to these impulses to reassert both the rule of law and the right accorded to all individuals. In *McCleskey v. Kemp* Justice Brennan's dissenting opinion observes, "Those whom we would banish from society or from the human community itself often speak in too faint a voice to be heard above society's demand for punishment. It is the particular role of the courts to hear those voices, for the Constitution declares that the majoritarian chorus may not alone dictate the conditions of social life."[11] The law must stand outside the impulse for revenge and engage only in judicious punishment if the rule of law is to persist. Note that these arguments admit that the thirst for revenge is real and strong, yet they share the faith that the law can substitute for these passions and restore universal right. A law that punishes to reassert right, not to instill fear of the sovereign or to express the outrage of the people, is considered the clearest indication of the ability of law to constrain and govern political power.

But others, following in the tradition of Nietzsche, assert that state-administered punishment is merely the codification and formalization of the right of revenge. State punishment is an extension of the group cohesion that results from an expression of the natural desire for revenge. One dominant theme in punishment literature examines how the process of punishment is used as a tool of social cohesion. Which groups are exorcised and punished? What society criminalizes is often a method of governing the boundaries of membership. As soon as someone strays outside of accepted behavioral norms, punishment is wielded to increase compliance. But being able to punish is also a privilege of belonging in the group itself.

In Shirley Jackson's story "The Lottery," village members all gather together excitedly for what initially appears to be a sort of festival or raffle. One woman is randomly selected, and the rest of the village then stones her. Social cohesion is built through the active prosecution and exclusion of others—the rewards of group membership become crystal clear at such a moment. Those who punish are reaffirmed as members of the community. The power of the community is expressed when it punishes; the members of the community bond through their imposition of pain upon outsiders. In Jackson's story, there is no need for a crime, either real or imagined; it is the practice itself that breeds cohesion. "The Lottery" starkly conveys this message, but the same story is told by studies that show those who are most fearful of crime are least susceptible to it. The impulse to punish or exclude need not be rooted in any specific experience of victimization.

Any school playground in the world would reveal the cohesion of social groups through punishment and exclusion; punishment is necessary for the existence of the group, not because of the inevitability of crime. However, this example of the schoolyard suggests an important distinction between punishment conducted by social groups and the state. Unlike schoolchildren, the modern state does not punish simply because it can—rather, it must punish in the name of a value or ideal.

While group cohesion certainly can result from and even be the key motivation behind state punishment, I find the relationship between the act of punishing and the stated ideal most intriguing. The juxtaposition between pursuing a greater good and administering some sort of pain is improbable, difficult, and revealing.

Punishment and Political Order is not attempting to displace the sociological analysis of punishment but to supplement it. Social dynamics unquestionably impact the practices of state punishment. However, so do the stated ideals of a polity. I propose that practices of punishment force institutional powers and social groups to contend with political ideals. Punishment is where the ideals of a polity come to be dramatically situated in close proximity with the realities of governance, and thereby it provides the most difficult case in the expression of political order. Can a state appear just, even as it administers pain?

The answer to this question depends upon two different components. The first is the perception of those within the political order. There is no empirical distinction between the exercise of tyranny and the administration of punishment; it is entirely a matter of perception. Punishment seems to provide a strong catalyst for reflection upon the government; it draws attention to the exclusive prerogatives of state power, and to the vulnerabilities of citizens before this power. For this reason, dissatisfaction, dissent, or mere discomfort with a regime can frequently appear or be mobilized around practices of punishment. Punishment can cause fissures within the polity to grow, or it can create martyrs, solidifying a perception of betrayal by the state. A central theme throughout the chapters that follow is exploring the cultivation and evolution of these perceptions around state punishment as an integral element in political order—and its undoing.

It is simple to say that a polity is committed to justice; the difficulty comes in whether it is able to demonstrate that commitment to justice even in the administration of pain. If a regime cannot offer some rationale—whether that be service to God, impartial courts, the light of reason, or the necessity of power—and thereby convincingly assert that the administration of pain serves justice, state punishment becomes simply the exercise of brutality by one person over another with less power. No wonder the question of punishment plays such a prominent role in political theories throughout history: if punishment is mere opportunism, then political ideals can be nothing other than a flimsy scrim masking oppression. Can the exercise of state power, even at its most extreme, serve an ideal?

Political order offers the possibility that human beings can construct an earthly system that redeems our existence. One common aspect of all religious orders is that they offer an understanding of suffering as redemption. As soon as states punish in their own name, not that of God, then they have taken on a task of great magnitude. Political orders that administer suffering in the form of punishment must also promise redemption from this pain through the realization of a greater ideal (explored more fully in chapters 1,2, and 7, this volume). This study has forced me to consider whether political orders have established an impossible task for themselves: can an earthly order really redeem human suffering? Is the punishment done in the name of worldly ideals too difficult to justify? While it is often argued that the desire to limit state power is what created liberalism and its emphasis upon the sanctity of individual rights and bodies, all liberal regimes make exceptions in the case of punishment. Justifying punishment by relating it to some kind of idealism is a dynamic in all political orders. Punishment demands the most precise balance between serving an ideal and serving power.

Studying both the history and present exercise of state punishment suggests that most regimes are not up to this difficult task. The prerogatives of power hold an irresistible allure, and I doubt very much whether any instance of state punishment is completely devoted to ideals of justice. In fact, I have come to wonder whether the pivotal role that punishment must play in secular political systems is one of the most enduring weaknesses in any modern regime. To administer pain in the name of worldly ideals requires the sort of discipline and justification that could never be achieved consistently. Consider, for example, the juxtaposition of Aristotle's claim that the state must punish to reassert the good with his knowledge of the trial of Socrates. You could argue that Aristotle was defining an ideal as a response to this travesty of justice; on the other hand, you could argue that just punishment is an impossible standard to uphold. Though the rewards, redemption, and punishments of the afterlife are impossible to discern, judge, and debate, the costs, pain, and problems of earthly punishment are readily available for us to question. Secular states must be able to punish in their own name, but this fact is nonetheless the Achilles' heel of any regime. Punishment provides the foundations of political order, but they are invariably Manichaean.

The seven chapters that follow move from the largest theoretical issues of politics and order to more specific case studies in contemporary American politics while pursuing two central themes. The first is punishment as a central problem for a political regime: how can a state, charged with the protection of a people, administer pain? Many of the most distinctive features of modern political governance have been developed in managing this paradoxical prerogative. The definition of sovereignty, the stated relationship between idealism and pragmatism in the administration of a regime, and the movement of redemption into the political realm are three methods that have allowed states to legitimate practices of punishment.

The second unifying theme in my discussion is the ever-shifting relationship between a regime and a given population that makes up the most essential element in any political order. Punishment uniquely reveals this dynamic element of political order. While state punishment normally demonstrates the ability of a regime to administer a population, it can at times also be destabilizing, creating resistance to and critique of a regime. Many studies of punishment have concentrated on the first dynamic, but they have neglected the potential for change that can arise as a result of punishment that is perceived as illegitimate.

Chapter 1, "The Whip of Utopia: On Punishment and Political Vision," introduces both themes through utopian and dystopian political visions. Sir Thomas More's *Utopia* is framed by discussions of penal practices in sixteenth-century England, leading into a comparison with the more pragmatic Utopians who enslave their criminals to do necessary public works. More helps us to understand how punishment serves as a means by which to understand the constant negotiation between the needs of political administration and the aims of justice. Franz Kafka's "In the Penal Colony" presents a decidedly dystopian vision of punishment, relating it to the pursuit of ideals as well. Both More's and Kafka's works present instances of punishment to stimulate a response in their readers, displaying the crucial elements of audience and perception in the development of just punishment and political regimes.

The second chapter, "'Man's Life Is but a Prison': Human Reason, Secular Political Order, and the Punishments of God," explores the movement of suffering and redemption from the religious realm into the political one through *The Book of Job* and Hobbes's *Leviathan*. In the Bible, human suffering was explained as a punishment from God, thus bestowing a logic to pain as well as offering the hope that such pain will be redemptive. Hobbes takes up the challenge of Job and creates a state that will make human suffering conformable to human logic. However, this shift means that state punishments also need to provide the hope of redemption, something that is exceedingly difficult to achieve. Hence, punishment both demonstrates and provides the catalyst for the secularization of human order but displays how unstable the foundations of this order can be.

In chapter 3, "Earthly Divinity: Punishment and the Requirements of Sovereignty," I investigate the development of modern conceptions of sovereignty. The odd combination of immanence and transcendence in the modern state can be viewed in light of state punishment, and in fact, this combination is one of the central ways of legitimating such punishment. The connections with the previous chapter are apparent, as sovereignty is a trace element of the divine that survives in secular political regimes.

Chapter 4, "Severing the Sanguinary Empire: Punishment and Early American Democratic Idealism," explores the early American republic and the role that punishment played in the struggle to break from England's colonial empire and in the definition of the new state. This chapter demonstrates the potential relationship between idealism and punishment most clearly—a connection which seems exceptionally weak today. The contrast between this early democratic idealism and the subject of chapter 5, "Punishment in Liberal Regimes," which explores classical liberal political thought and the contemporary penal regime in the United States, could not be more stark. Here I look at liberal exceptionalism in terms of the punishment that is at the foundations of liberal thought. Punishment has always served a particularly important role in the development of liberal principles such as responsibility and personhood. The social contract regime, based upon notions that are simultaneously concrete yet ethereal, requires punishment to make itself tangible. Understanding these elements in liberal political thought in part helps to explain what penal practices accomplish today in the United States, and why it is difficult to critique them on purely economic, racially unjust, or utilitarian grounds.

Chapter 6, "Hitched to the Post: Prison Labor, Choice, and Citizenship," continues my study of contemporary U.S. penal practices but links them to neoliberal economics. One of the most important and compelling strains of political analysis of punishment emphasizes its economic function. While I generally agree that there is a crucial political economic component, I present the cases of prison labor in an era of deindustrialization to argue that the connection is not always straight-forward. Prison labor is not utilized to extract labor—in fact, it is generally spectacularly unproductive—but rather is a mechanism for enforcing the presumptions of neoliberalism. Though focused on different aspects of current politics, both chapters 5 and 6 help explain the relationship between penal practices and liberal ideals of individuality, contract, and freedom in the United States. Though the penal system is anything but egalitarian, nor does it promote individual liberties, it needs to be viewed in relation to liberal idealism, not as a deviation from it.

Finally, chapter 7, "Punishment and the Spiral of Disorder," is an exploration of punishment as a destabilizing force in contemporary U.S. international politics. This conclusion is more suggestive than comprehensive, as this topic deserves a full-length exploration. I include this discussion to examine how punishment can play a crucial role in international as well as domestic regimes, and also as a sober reminder that an unjust penal regime can reach over oceans and touch the lives of citizens of other regimes. The exposure of prisoner abuse in Abu Ghraib, the continuing discussions of prisoner treatment in Guantánamo Bay and Afghanistan, and the revelation of secret prisons in Eastern Europe have catalyzed world opinion against the U.S. government, as would be predicted by the arguments in the rest of the book. The dynamics of perception and the awareness first introduced in chapter 1 become especially important here. Perhaps the most revealing perspective one can gain on practices of punishment is from the eyes of an outsider. Would you want such practices to become emblematic of your regime? The fictional scenarios spun by More and Kafka have come to fruition, as punishment has come to represent the regime of the United States in an unfavorable light. Partly out of discomfort with this fact, American support of the country's missions abroad and the aims of the War on Terror measurably waned with the publicizing of the abuse. Illegitimate use of the power to punish can backfire, leading to a depletion of legitimacy and hence the power of command.

Let me conclude with one final reason to rescue the relationship between political idealism and punishment. After all, we have no way to evaluate the ethics or inherent justice of systems of punishment if we do not remember that punishment is supposed to be an expression of justice, not merely power. When we focus on institutional practices of punishment, or sociological accounts of punishment and membership, we look at punishment as a practice of power. While it is certainly that, it is also linked to the ideals inherent in a political order. This book addresses the lacunae in the literature by presenting the central role that punishment plays in different seminal works of political theory. I do so not to replace the other readings of punishment that are more familiar but to complement them. For this reason, this text, while dwelling primarily upon these works of political theory, will also bring in these sociological, economic, and historical studies of punishment. Seeing how theories of punishment relate to practices of punishment reveals a central dialectic in politics—the struggle between ideal and real. And to bring up these idealistic foundations of punishment is not to fit a flowered glove over an iron fist but to have a firmer understanding of exactly what we betray when we engage in practices of punishment that are inherently unjust.

CHAPTER 1

The Whip of Utopia

On Punishment and Political Vision

He who will not listen must feel.
    —German proverb

Utopias and dystopias amplify the powerful ambiguity of all political philosophy as thinking that nonetheless tries to accomplish change. They are fictional accounts that are deliberately ahistorical and present dreams or nightmares—not manifestos that demand action. As Judith Shklar notes, "It is a vision not of the probable but of the 'not-impossible.'" We tend to dismiss utopian visions as fantastic or idealistic to a fault: a proposal that is labeled "utopian" is not destined for realization. Paradoxically, the limitations of utopias as blueprints provide their political salience. Utopias present a viewpoint unmarred by history or necessity; in contrast to utopia "all historical actuality is here brought to judgment . . . and found wanting."[1] The power of utopian writing springs from the careful presentation of contrast: contrast between the culture being presented and the reader's and/or writer's own, and between idealism and practicality. Dystopias also bring a shock of recognition through comparison. Here is a distasteful vision. What elements of this picture can be found in your own world?

In this chapter, I look at two pieces of writing from remarkably different ages and orientations that fulfill the political function of utopias and dystopias: Sir Thomas More's *Utopia* and Franz Kafka's "In the Penal Colony." The parallels between the two pieces are striking, even though the tone of each work could not be more different. Travelers cross cultural and political boundaries and present their wisdom to an audience. The message of each is sufficiently ambiguous and uncomfortable to propel a shift in perception on the part of their readers. Both texts frame their message by focusing on practices of punishment. Here I will explain how this thematic focus is closely related to the overall

17

purpose of both texts to shift the political consciousness of their audience. Punishment allows More and Kafka to mobilize their readers: how will you respond to this exercise of power? What practices of state power do you accept as given, and why? Furthermore, examining practices of punishment displays how a regime itself negotiates between the demands of rule and the pursuit of justice. Both utopian thought and punishment serve as a catalyst: they offer the pointed opportunity for reflection and critique. How do we judge the exercise of power in relation to its larger ideals, and how are we to respond, given this newly found awareness?

More and Kafka both drive home the message that political orders are contingent upon the proclivities, not only of their rulers, but also of the population at large. An outside perspective stirs our consciousness; we evaluate the strange world being presented, but then, ideally, we turn these trained eyes onto our own systems and start to consider what an outsider would say. Punishment as the central theme in both of these texts helps to intensify this process of political reeducation in a number of ways.

First of all, it brings the incomplete nature of political regimes into sharp focus. The basic task of political order is to create harmony out of what is a volatile and varied population. For this reason, the unruly aspects of human existence are rarely glimpsed in tracts of political philosophy and most works of political science today. Political philosophy is often engaged in composing systems that neutralize or eliminate human imperfections; recent political science strives for empiricism and predictive capabilities, hence the out of the ordinary is "controlled" or registered in "standard deviations." Nonetheless, anything involving human beings strays from the ideal-type. Political orders invariably contain ideals that are imperfectly realized: therefore a clash between ideal and empirical is bound to occur. Even if our theories and models do not acknowledge this chasm, political regimes must find some way of dealing with the troubling propensity of human beings to nonconformity. This gap between human behavior and political ideals is occupied by state punishment. The nagging reality that accompanies the impulse to political idealism is the mortality and bodily existence of human beings. The body that desires, bleeds, kills, and dies is the inescapable ground of human life: it administers and requires punishment to bring it into line with the promise of order. Punishment is where the ideal of perfect administration collides with our moral and material weakness. It is one thing to have an ideal, another thing alto-gether to realize it. Emphasizing this difficulty allows both More and Kafka to deny their readers the simple denigration of the real in favor of the ideal; instead they are forced to reckon with the need to balance both aspects in a regime.

Second, punishment not only points toward the unrealized promise of political order; it also provokes the question, What efforts to realize an ideal are appropriate? More and Kafka both present punishment as an expression of a regime's ideals, not just its brute powers. From the perspective of an outsider as provided by More and Kafka, we recon-sider accepted forms of punishment and are forced to judge which practices are truly appropriate in the name of realizing ideals. As Corey Robin points out in *Fear: The History of a Political Idea,* the horrors of the twentieth century have led us to regard idealism with suspicion. Total-itarian regimes are commonly blamed upon "ideas that cast death . . . as a way, the way, of life."[2] George Kateb describes a similar dynamic in his essay "The Adequacy of the Canon," arguing that what he terms the "hyperactive imagination" is culpable for the mass atrocities of the twentieth century. He describes the hyperactive imagination as "the rabid capacity to make the present absent, to imagine a different reality, to have designs on that reality."[3] What characterizes this imaginative capacity is the ability to see a vision of what can be to the complete exclusion of what is, combined with the drive to turn that vision into reality. While Kateb's examples are extreme, which is appropriate to his task of explaining the catastrophes of our times, this dynamic is present in the more mundane acts of state punishment, as both More and Kafka make clear. Most people would regard killing, maiming, or depriving personal freedom in the name of an ideal with considerable suspicion. Yet this is precisely what states do when they punish. Clearly individual rights are subordinated to some ideals today, no matter how fervently we think we distrust this sort of activity.

But Robin's observation about the ideologically wary population of the early twenty-first century prods me to argue that the other option—relinquishing any ideal at all—is just as tragic. If idealism leads to egre-gious actions, it is tempting to conclude that it is simply a dangerous element in politics. Should we do no more than embrace order for the mere sake of order? I don't think so. Clearly the correct balance must be a dedication to ideals that is not myopic, and a willingness to envision alternatives while acknowledging material preconditions and limitations, which ultimately is the message presented by *Utopia* and "In the Penal Colony."[4]

Both texts are deliberately disorienting, helping us to see that the question of how to relate political ideals and a given population cannot be definitively resolved; rather, it is the negotiation between the two that composes political citizenship. In these texts, and in our lives, punishment provides a clear forum for the negotiation between rights and pragmatism and the cultivation of legitimacy and stability for a political regime. By making these points through the presentation of punishment, both More and Kafka bring an urgency to our ability to grasp these dilemmas of political thought. In punishment, the ethereal debates about theory and practice contained in virtually all tracts of political philosophy fall to the ground in a most spectacular fashion; questions of principle and right become ones of life and flesh.

Punishment in Utopia

In a letter, Erasmus reported that Sir Thomas More had initially written only the second book of *Utopia* that described the practices and society of the Utopians but then later wrote the first "because it was needed." So rather than being a straightforward account of a fictive society, there are two different worlds represented in *Utopia*, and it is in the juxtaposition of the two that the book's central themes and brilliance are achieved.

Sir Thomas More's *Utopia* begins by setting the stage of Raphael Hythloday's detailed account of the political and social order of Utopia. Thomas More is in Flanders during a journey for the business of state, when his friend Peter Giles introduces him to Raphael Hythloday, who has traveled the world and combines the wisdom of a philosopher and the scientism of an explorer. The second book is the traveler's account of Utopia; the first book is a dialogue between Giles, More, and Hythloday that frames the story of the second.

The themes of the first book are complex, but two important elements emerge from the seemingly secondary introduction. The first is that Hythloday is established as a reliable source, unsullied by service to any of the powers that be, in marked contrast to More himself who is in Flanders serving the Crown. This is one of the most central problems for anyone interested in political reform: only those subject to a political order would be motivated to reform it, but they lack the perspective to know what the alternatives are. The purpose of utopian works is to insert the outside perspective into a given political context, thus achieving a destabilization of perception. Greatly impressed by Hythloday's acute observations and knowledge of different political orders, the narrator, More, wonders, "why do you not enter into the service of some king . . . this learning of yours and your knowledge of peoples and places would not only serve to delight him but would also make you fit to inform him."[5] Hythloday recoils at the suggestion saying he would not want to be enslaved by any king. A king's ear is deaf to all but the counsel he seeks, and Hythloday would prefer to be pursuing the truth than currying favor.

When Peter Giles first introduces Hythloday to More, he tells him he is a voyager "like Plato," immediately linking his geographical wisdom with the same remove as the philosopher. Plato wanted philosophers to rule, because they would ensure the persistent impact and enlightened judgment of the outside perspective. Quentin Skinner has discussed this dynamic in More's *Utopia* and termed it the *problem of counsel*. Hythloday uses this interchange as an example of his unwillingness to compromise, and how this truthfulness would be poorly received by rulers. The struggle over counsel and politics is also autobiographical: Skinner reports that More had agreed to go into the service of Henry VIII immediately before writing the book.[6] Though Hythloday insists that he is not to be corrupted by service to actual powers, the text of *Utopia* suggests otherwise. Hythloday's indignant protestations can be read as signaling that the suggestions that follow are uncorrupted by proximity to power. After his cantankerous pronouncement regarding the state's creation of thieves, Hythloday's powerful listeners *do* entertain alternative notions of punishment. And while the first book of *Utopia* insists that princes spurn wise counselors and vice versa, the second book plainly offers Hythloday's services by recounting his story. Hythloday's perspective as an outsider makes him bring reformatory ideas to English penal practices, but it also establishes to the reader the necessity of seeing one's order from the outside. More points out the paradox that guides his utopian project: only the wisdom of outsiders can provoke this kind of self-reflection and the potential for reform.

The content of this debate over the relationship between wisdom and ruling is punishment. As an example of the myopic wisdom of rulers, Hythloday recounts a conversation with the Archbishop of Canterbury and one of the king's counselors about the practice of hanging thieves. The counselor lauded the rigorous application of the principles of justice: "They were executed everywhere, he said, sometimes as many as twenty at a time hanging on one gallows, and he remarked that he was all the more amazed that the country was cursed to have so many of them prowling about everywhere, since so few escaped punishment."[7]

Hythloday disagrees with this assessment and offers an enlarged view of the problem of thievery including the shortage of land (his famous sheep-eat-men observation), the learned incompetence of the middlemen who administer the feudal orders, the markets for beef and wool, the desire for luxurious living, and the presence of gambling houses that leave many in desperate ruin. The bodies that litter the state's gallows could not be pulled down quickly enough to make room for more under such circumstances.

> Certainly unless you remedy these evils, it is pointless for you to boast of the justice administered in the punishment of thieves, a justice which is specious rather than either just or expedient. In fact when you bring people up with the worst sort of education and allow their morals to be corrupted little by little from their earliest years, and then punish them at last as grown men when they commit the crimes which from childhood they have given every prospect of committing, what else are you doing, I ask you, but making them into thieves and then punishing them for it?[8]

The crime has nothing whatsoever to do with the punishment but instead results from social organization.

More scholar George Logan has observed that the debate about punishment aptly establishes the primary themes of *Utopia*.[9] In commenting that the practice of hanging thieves is neither just nor expedient, Hythloday introduces the central question of *Utopia*, and indeed virtually all political thought, by asking how best to reconcile the needs of practicality and justice. Hanging thieves, since it fails to prevent thievery *and* is a betrayal of the principle of proportionality in punishment, fits neither criterion. While it is tempting to assume that More is building the ideal with little attention to the practical, in actuality *Utopia* offers a more nuanced message on this problematic, which becomes clear when contrasting the penal practices of little value in England with the penal practices of Utopia.

To introduce a utopian vision by discussing punishment seems counterintuitive to say the least, so we expect to encounter a rapid shift from the critique implied in the first book to a more idyllic political vision in the second. But the unsavory elements of More's discussion persist even in the second book of *Utopia*, when we have presumably moved from the corrupted European order to the Utopian one. Hythloday has commented that inequalities of wealth and property create crime, along with an undue love of luxury. Utopia has eliminated wealth, luxury, and property yet still has to conduct punishments. If Hythloday's prognosis in the first book were to hold true, in such a perfectly engineered society there would be no need for punishment. Nevertheless, we find slavery in Utopia. Rather than killing criminals, Utopians enslave them, and they perform many of the menial tasks upon which their society is absolutely dependent. Prisoners wear differently colored clothing for quick recognition and must devote their lives in public service to amend for the harms caused to the community by their crimes.

There are three classes of slaves: those who were condemned to death in other countries and sent to Utopia where they can instead labor their days away; the poor of other countries who presumably come to Utopia and request to be their slaves since such an existence is better than the life offered to them in their own countries; and finally the Utopians who have committed crimes. "Utopian slaves, however, they treat more harshly since they consider them baser and deserving of more severe punishment because they had an extraordinary education and the best moral training, yet still could not be restrained from moral wrongdoing."[10]

Hythloday points out with apparent delight the practicality of this system of punishment: all benefit from their labor when none would profit from their execution. The public slaves also serve as a countermonument. He compares the criminals in chains to the statues of local heroes: they both serve as an incentive for citizens to become virtuous. If slaves can prove that "they regret the sin more than the punishment" the sentence can be ended, commuted by the rulers or by popular vote.[11] This comment reveals an understanding of the complexities of state punishment. This penitence is no simple task to discern or to produce. For virtually everyone who is punished is quite sorry indeed that they have been caught, but very few become truly remorseful of their crime.

One paradox of punishment is that the pain is supposed to encourage reform and recognition of personal duty. On the contrary, those being punished are more likely to blame those administering the pain for their misfortunes. Acceptance of personal responsibility for the crime would require that the person being punished give more legitimacy to the law and its executioners than to their personal choices or comfort. Hythloday's account of punishment in Utopia quickly discards these subtleties. If the slaves refuse to labor and are disruptive "they are finally slaughtered like wild beasts." So much for the inherent worth of man and the promise of just social order whereby individuals combine together, sometimes giving up their individual gain for collective good.

The international order of Utopia is no less troubling. The Utopians are a peace-loving people, so they hire mercenaries to fight their wars so as not to stain their own population with wanton bloodletting. As self-proclaimed peaceniks, we might assume they fight only in self-defense, but they invade other countries who may have insulted their friends, countries who treat their citizens badly (and who might be happier as slaves in Utopia), or countries that *might* threaten their interests. Ultimately, Utopia sounds imperialistic. Shlomo Avineri has commented upon these unappealing aspects of Utopia, concluding, "Utopian thinking never really maintains that the given human nature is perfect; on the contrary, it has to be purged and cleansed from its intrinsic evil."[12] In Avineri's view, Utopia is created as "perfect" by its ruthless excision of anything that is less than perfect—wars are fought on other turf and by soldiers from other countries, slaves become the repository of the population's moral failings—their public display asserts the relative morality of everyone else. The problem with Avineri's reading is that it replicates the simplistic understanding of crime and punishment that Hythloday explicitly rejects in the first book of *Utopia.* More does not think you can eliminate thievery by killing thieves; instead you must look into the inherent causes of criminality. In Hythloday's view, Utopia does all it can to prevent criminality through the eradication of property and wealth and by creating the best possible system of education. Nonetheless, More remarks to Hythloday, "For everything will not be done well until all men are good, and I do not expect to see that for quite a few years yet."[13] The only available strategy is to balance the needs of practicality and justice and to create the best possible arrangements for cultivating virtue and achiev-

ing stability. The social organization dispenses with all the requirements of justice; those people that persist in falling outside the utopic
order can be punished in the way that is most expedient.

If this is the case, then punishment is far more central to *Utopia* than
it first appears, and in fact, displays the central problem of the book.
What do you do with the failings of humans in even the most perfect of
social orders? In less than perfect orders, the state can be blamed, at
least in part. But there are convicts even in Utopia. On the one hand, we
could take the presence of punishment as a sign of freedom, rather than
failure, within the administered world of Utopia. After all, as opposed
to other forms of social control, such as conditioning, propaganda, or
peer pressure, using punishment to maintain order "maximizes individual freedom within the coercive framework of law."[14] Individuals
have a choice whether to obey the law, and punishment is a form of
control that is deferred until a transgression has actually occurred.

On the other hand, Hythloday observes the rage that erupts when
this bestowed freedom is abused. The fury of the Utopians was
reserved for the betrayal of their own perfection by members of the
society. These deviants prove the inevitable incompleteness of political
order; no matter how beautifully constructed a society is there will
always be those who fall outside of the boundaries. Perfection, defined
as the ability to construct a society where justice is fully realized, is a
mirage; the real test of a society is how it manages its failures. This is
why *Utopia* begins with a discussion of criminality, and why the pressing question of political order is not simply the ideal, but how to relate
the ideal with the pragmatic. The final answer is clearly not offered
here in *Utopia*, and More suggests that it never can be—the matter is left
open for debate at every point in the book.

The message of *Utopia* is that a perfect reconciliation of justice and
expediency is not possible, therefore how the state decides to punish
reveals where it falls in juggling the two elements. I agree with others
who have suggested that *Utopia* ultimately argues that there is no way
to engineer a perfect convergence of justice and practicality.[15] The thematic of punishment becomes central in the text because this is exactly
where states are forced to try this negotiation. Yet punishment also cir-
cles back to the first theme I introduced here, and that is the wisdom of
outsiders. In the cases of both England and Utopia, observers recount
their official practices of punishment, opening both regimes to examination. More wants us to adopt the outsider position and turn back to

question English penal practices as representative of the character and purpose of the regime. Does a government feast upon its unfortunate? Does it profit from criminality and thus secretly cultivate it? Does it take too much pleasure in disciplining the bodies of criminals or viewing their misery? Every political order has stated ideals and beliefs, but practices of punishment reveal whether and how these ideals are betrayed. Conversely, ideals, when followed absolutely, can be just as problematic. Is outrage too vehement? Do we lynch in the name of our own righteousness? More suggests that we need to discard the examples of both the English and the Utopians, and balance idealism and practicality in punishment. For instance, a country would never throw everyone who sped on a highway into jail for criminality; on the other hand, it would create chaos to give up trying to regulate traffic. The negotiation between practicality and principle is played out over and over in choices about why, how, and whether to punish crimes.

As the reported discussion between Hythloday and the Archbishop of Canterbury in the first book suggests, another central issue in determining practices of punishment is how responsibility is perceived. What is so startling about seeing this debate articulated in 1516 is that it is the same one that we have today. Does the amount of criminality have any relation to the punishments administered, or does it have more to do with social conditions outside the law? There is a series of relationships implied here: in one view, the crime incurs the punishment; the causal relationship exists in the frame of reference of individual choice. Failure to punish harshly would send the message that the crime is not deserving of punishment, severing the causal link. Crime would then run rampant. This view assumes that the criminal always has a good incentive to break the law, and that punitive pain must outweigh the calculated advantage.

The other viewpoint, here represented by Hythloday, sees the causal relationship existing in a different frame of reference: social conditions create the crime. If social conditions are such that either a true or perceived advantage is derived from crime, then the social order has simply failed. Society must be organized in such a way that there is no gain from participating in criminal activity. Until this level of social engineering has been achieved, the need to punish must be perceived as a failure on the part of the state in accomplishing its mission, not necessarily a failure on the part of the criminal.

This debate signals why the assumptions about individual responsibility that support practices and conceptions of punishment are so difficult. If we assume that people are malleable enough to be trained, then why suddenly assume that their choices are individual? More observes that the special fury of the state is reserved for those people who bite the hand that trained and fed them: "After all I've done for you, see what you have done!" The structures of punishment insist we are individuals, but political order assumes we are educable citizens. One aspect of determining the role of punishment in political order is the negotiation between persistent human unpredictability and the promise of social administration. Practices of punishment are one arena where societies are forced to grapple with the fact that human beings are conditioned yet free.

Punishment as a practice is particularly salient: it represents, as I have said, much about how a regime deals with its failings. More also makes it clear that the population participates in these given structures through their acceptance or questioning of them. Today, we as readers are outsiders to both regimes that More describes in *Utopia*, hence it is much easier for us to be critical of them. Those subject to a political system are most likely to accept its practices. Utopia offers the view from the outside as an impetus to reform. But More makes it plain that the prisoners described in both regimes provide another cause for reflection—they are the internal dissidents to the established order as well as the products of that regime's failure. In other words, those being punished and those viewing the punishment fall outside the regime's common preconceptions of proper order, thereby harboring the potential for critique and change. Of course, those being punished have none of the legitimacy or dispassion of the observers, and they have guilt, not objectivity on their side.

In the Penal Colony

Dystopias can be read as companion volumes to utopias, and indeed viewing Kafka's "In the Penal Colony" alongside More's *Utopia* provokes many of the same considerations of audience, idealism, political order, and punishment. Franz Kafka's fictional work provides a crystalline vision of politics by taking the familiar elements of our administration of justice and placing them in an unfamiliar context or by magnifying common assumptions or trends. Kafka's work is often fantastic in form, but his intent was worldly. His dreamlike narratives push readers to recognize the world as it actually is, not as it is commonly perceived. In a conversation with Gustav Janouch, Kafka described his work as follows: "The dream reveals the reality, which conception lags behind. That is the horror of life—the terror of art."[16] It isn't that Kafka creates dreamlike worlds; instead his work brings out the surreal aspects of our own. Kafka's bizarre yet straightforward descriptions penetrate his readers who then carry that sense of estrangement into their own experiences. Those who have read *The Trial* will never sanguinely face a bureaucratic maze again; those who read his story "In the Penal Colony" will respond to the phrase "sentenced to death" with a shudder. Jane Bennett has written about Kafka's work as a contribution to political thought, arguing that he writes genealogical stories that "highlight the contingent elements of an ideal, or its falsifications, or the arbitrary devaluations and exclusions that accompany it, or the incompatible elements within it."[17] "In the Penal Colony" shakes our perception of the relationship between punishment, justice, and enlightenment to the very core. I can think of no better place than Kafka to start unraveling common assumptions about punishment and politics.

The narrator of the story is an explorer who is visiting a penal colony. He is apparently someone of stature, as all the administrators in the colony assume that he shall report back on their activities and that his opinions shall carry some weight. Most of the story takes place with four characters around a machine in a deserted area of a penal colony. The officer is showing the explorer a machine invented by the original Commandant of the colony; the two main characters are accompanied by the condemned and the soldier who is guarding the prisoner. The officer is preparing the machine for the condemned, who failed to obey his orders: over the course of twelve hours, the machine will write the sentence "Honor Thy Superiors" over the body of the man repeatedly. The machine is carefully designed to inscribe the sentence upon the condemned, literally. The mechanism is carefully designed to kill its victims, but very slowly and with great precision. The officer observes that at the sixth hour, "Enlightenment comes to the most dull-witted. It begins around the eyes. From there it radiates. A moment that might tempt one to get under the Harrow oneself."[18] Most courts simply proclaim the sentence or judgment; here the punishment inscribes the judgment onto the body of the prisoner. The Officer points out that after the Harrow's work is done, it can truly be said that "the judgment has been fulfilled."

The story begins with the observation, "It's a remarkable piece of apparatus." In life, Kafka was employed by a Worker's Accident Insurance Company to calculate the risk of employments in mechanical and industrial occupations.[19] One can imagine that the story might have had inspiration from the claims of actual workers. At any rate, Kafka's own occupational experience is on display as he takes pages to explain the intricate workings of the machine: the engineering precision required to inscribe the sentence upon the body of the prisoner without killing him or her is indeed truly breathtaking. Wool and cotton pads dab away at the skin of the prisoner after each inscription of the sentence upon his skin. This promotes cleaner scarring, making the sentence legible for those attending the proceeding. They have gone to great lengths to concoct a system of punishment that is precise, deliberate, and exact. The punishment is the exact realization of the sentence; the punishment consists of the moral to be learned. The Harrow is the product of generations of technological and medical knowledge: it is both the brutal product and grim instrument of human enlightenment. Hegel's view of just punishment as reestablishing the proportional and exactly calibrated to the crime is monstrously achieved here.

It is important that the story's narrator be an outsider, someone who is neither subject to nor required to administer the system of justice in the penal colony, in order to share in the reader's horror as the machine and its purpose are revealed. As outsiders, both the explorer and reader offer the possibility of clear evaluation and critique of deformed practices of justice and punishment. The political brilliance of the story is the fact that Kafka denies the explorer and the reader any easy judgments. As Walter Benjamin observed, Kafka's goals of changing the consciousness of his readers is accomplished by presenting the tragic events of individuals—for instance, turning into a bug or being investigated for no clear reason—in a context where "everything continues as usual."[20] Can we, the readers, continue with our lives when confronted with the brutality of these practices? If so, we become as complicit as the figures in the story that administer death with the ease of habit and the scaffolding of legitimacy.

The officer explains the workings of the machine with unflappable zeal. The mechanical descriptions are punctuated with explanations of overcoming manifold difficulties to achieve perfection in the machinery: "So that the actual progress of the sentence can be watched, the Harrow is made of glass. Getting the needles fixed in the glass was a

technical problem, but after many experiments we overcame the difficulty. No trouble was too great for us to take, you see" (147). The enthu-
siasm and precision of the officer's description matches the mechanism
of the machine: both seem bizarrely juxtaposed to the practice of torture.

Suddenly, the officer begins to beg the explorer for assistance: now
that the old Commandant is dead, the new Commandant refuses to
order the parts necessary for the maintenance of the machine. The
machine of perfect justice and enlightenment is thereby threatened, as
its mechanisms grow creaky. At first, the officer sounds like a bureaucrat frustrated in the accomplishment of his appointed task—he cannot
service the machine properly. "Now he has taken charge of the
machine money himself, and if I send for a new strap they ask for the
old strap as evidence, and the new strap takes ten days to appear and
then is of shoddy material and not much good. But how I am supposed
to work the machine without a strap, that's something nobody bothers
about" (151). Kafka's officer predates Arendt's Adolf Eichmann by
forty-nine years but demonstrates the same bureaucratic exertions
behind grisly murder.

However, the reader slowly starts to understand that the officer is a
true believer in the machine, not a mindless servant of it. He believes in
the machine as both a product of and impetus for human accomplishment. Through the machine he can help change the world, not merely
administer it. The old Commandant was not content to be exiled with
criminals in a penal colony; he worked tirelessly to devise a way to
reform and redeem those that had been given up by the mother country. The machine was designed to bring enlightenment to the penal
colony, mechanically lifting the most hopeless cases to the highest stage
of human consciousness. Arnold Weinstein has observed that the
machine in this story presents one solution to the fundamental problem
of language: "Language cannot *be* what it says."[21] Designing the
machine that solves this problem reveals an intensive familiarity with
the traditions of law and the Enlightenment, not an ignorance of them,
as we might be tempted to assume.

The opacity of language is the same problem in the law and the
founding of political orders generally.[22] The word or law cannot be the
world that it brings forth: it is the classical dilemma of political philosophers that idea and practice are distinct, they are always removed from
their object. Punishment is to bring the law, the imperative, into exis-

tence—to move it beyond the realm of mere language. The machine transforms the impotence of language into the force of understanding. The officer comments, "Our sentence does not sound severe," and indeed no law does until it is somehow realized. The punishment machine perfectly realizes the law and therefore serves as the head, heart, and soul of the colony, which, according to the officer, had been perfectly organized by the old Commandant. This is a person who cared about creating good in the world, and who believed in the per- fectibility of human beings through knowledge, technology, and polit- ical institutions.

The officer explains that originally the entire colony would turn out for the executions, people fighting for the privilege of watching it up close (the honor was awarded to children, naturally). "How we all absorbed the look of transfiguration on the face of the sufferer, how we bathed our cheeks in the radiance of that justice, achieved at last and fading so quickly!" (154). The past glory of the machine is a sad contrast to the colony and its machine as the explorer finds it. No one attends the executions, and the machine groans due to its neglect. Without pop- ular support and maintenance even a mechanism of perfect justice falls into disrepair. The officer wails at the explorer: "Do you realize the shame of it?" (155). He views the explorer as the last hope to resurrect the former glory of the mechanism and return justice to the colony.

When the explorer tells the officer that he will not support him in his attempts to save the machine and carry out the vision of the old Com- mandant, the officer frees the condemned man and places himself under the Harrow. He programs the machine to inscribe "Be Just!" on himself. The last true believer in the system proves his devotion by placing himself into its mechanisms. The machine starts to malfunction, and despite efforts by the explorer, the Harrow goes haywire and kills the officer. His rapid death denies him the torturous pleasure and the radiance of justice that he has thus far experienced only vicariously. The explorer regards the face on the officer's corpse: "It was as it had been in life; no sign was visible of the promised redemption; what the others had found in the machine the officer had not found; the lips were firmly pressed together, the eyes were open, with the same expression as in life, the look was calm and convinced, through the forehead went the point of the great iron spike" (166).

The ending of the story considerably complicates Kafka's message, which until now could be seen as a description of maniacal devotion to a deformed sense of justice. Closely followed by the soldier and the now freed condemned man, the explorer goes back into the town to find the new Commandant and report on the day's events, but instead finds the old Commandant's grave. It is hidden underneath tables in a teahouse; the other patrons move a table out of the way to reveal the state of the old Commandant's legacy. Inscripted upon his grave is the message, "Here rests the old Commandant. His adherents, who now must be nameless, have dug this grave and set up this stone. There is a prophecy that after a certain number of years the Commandant will rise again and lead his adherents from this house to recover the colony. Have faith and wait!" (167). Other patrons in the teahouse sneer at the message on the grave, and the explorer begins to recoil from the people around him. The belief in redemption sheltered by the officer and his Commandant has now disappeared from the colony, hidden under a table and brutally sacrificed in the Harrow. Those that remain are inarticulate, disbelieving.

The infuriating complexity and ultimate political significance of this story come from Kafka's refusal to provide a straightforward reference point. Initially the officer seems fanatical, and the condemned man, the lamb about to be sacrificed. Then the officer sacrifices himself, while the condemned man's face is animated by the cruelty of the machine. In contrast to the justice sought by the man in the Harrow—the officer who has programmed the machine to inscribe "Be Just" on his body—the newly freed man watches his sacrifice and responds, "So this was revenge. Although he himself had not suffered to the end, he was to be revenged to the end. A broad silent grin now appeared on his face and stayed there all the rest of the time" (163). The people in the tearoom sneer at the optimism of the grave's inscription and the notion of resurrection. In contrast, the idealism of the officer and old Commandant seems virtuous, even touchingly naive. They dared to believe in enlightenment for all people, even the most abject, here in exile. The dream of earthly redemption for the incorrigible might be better than simply waiting for them to die out on the edge of the world.

Having frustrated the simple condemnation of the officer and old Commandant, and denying the condemned man any redeeming qualities, Kafka then proceeds to refuse the explorer any moral credibility as well. After he sees the grave and the response of those around him, the distressed and confused explorer scurries in a panic toward the docks, not stopping to talk with the new Commandant, and manages to jump on a ship as it pulls away from shore. The soldier and condemned man grasp at him and try and follow him onto the boat; their actions beg the explorer to provide the second chance that the penal colony has not. Will he take on the mantle of redemption refused by the new Commandant and bring them with him? "They could have jumped into the boat, but the explorer lifted a heavy knotted rope from the floor boards, threatened them with it, and so kept them from attempting the leap" (167). The reader cannot help being relieved to join the explorer and leave the entire scene behind with this last sentence.

All of Kafka's writing provokes more questions than it answers. "In the Penal Colony" has many interpretations, many of which seem plausible. The problem, as Sander Gilman observed about Kafka's work, is that "it is infinitely rereadable and inherently uninterpretable because it is so very interpretable."[23] It reproduces what we bring to it: hence it makes sense that this story's interpretations reflect the times and proclivities of its readers. In 1968, Wilhelm Emrich saw that "In the Penal Colony" was about the passing of an older order and the birth of a new one.[24] Many readers have found Jewish, anti-Jewish, Christian, and anti-Christian messages in the text. More recently, for example, in 2001 Paul Peters claimed the story "may indeed ultimately and appropriately be read as a kind of master narrative of the 'primal scene' of colonialism itself."[25] Falling in line with this company of critics, I think that focusing on the act and interpretation of punishment in this story—which seems to be an entirely novel approach—is particularly revealing. However, I make this argument while agreeing with some of the earlier emphases: we should think about punishment here in relationship to the existence of penal colonies, religious or earthly redemption or the lack thereof, the passing of a regime, and our position as outsiders who can judge.

Clearly, there are religious elements in the story, as many critics have observed. The innocent officer dies, replacing his body with the one of the condemned, seemingly destroying the machine through his sacrifice. The spiritual father of the colony, one who "combines everything in himself . . . soldier, judge, mechanic, chemist, and draughtsman," lies in wait, declaring a return if the earthbound are faithful. Though many are engaged in arguing whether the story falls in line with Christian or Judaic impulses, Kafka considerably complicates the story as a religious one in a number of ways.[26]

Redemption everlasting isn't the product of the Harrow and its inscription: instead earthly illumination is. The recognition brought on by the machine is fleeting, since it is inevitably followed by death within six hours, but it seems significant that "enlightenment" with all of its philosophical, abstract, and disembodied overtones is the product of the torture device. Suffering is not rewarded in the next life but instead is the direct route to knowledge in this one. The officer who puts himself into the machine as a demonstration of his faith in it doesn't gain the desired effect: enlightenment comes only from pain, not belief. Kafka's story uses religious motifs, but sharp twists change the effect of these elements in the story: the Harrow provides redemption in this world, and thereby it is an integral element of the political system of the colony.

Recent observers have begun to note the colonial setting of the story instead of the religious motifs.[27] It is certainly plausible that Kafka was concerned with writing a commentary on colonialism, as research suggests he was greatly influenced by the experiences of his uncles working in the French efforts to colonize Panama.[28] What other critics have not suggested is that the setting in a penal colony is of particular importance, and more telling in the narrative than straightforward colonialism. Of course, penal colonies and colonialism were closely related endeavors (as I also explore in chapter 5). However, the rationale behind the penal colony was particularly incoherent. Penal colonies were developed in part for their economic utility in settling the globe. Yet they were also developed from a particular conundrum created by the rapid change in ideals and even regimes of governance in Western Europe. Penalties were more punitive than general predispositions were liable to support. Before the relatively high-cost penitentiary and prison options were developed, governments adopted exile as a more humane alternative to corporal and capital punishment. Convicts would be sent to designated penal colonies and then remain as settlers. The policy makes sense as a measure of making punishment more humane and also as a method to populate the globe with settlers from their nation. But the practice does not make sense at all from the ideological standpoint driving colonization—the civilizing mission—either through education, institutions, or religion, often attached to colonial enterprises. How are those deemed unfit for European citizenship supposed to provide for the cultivation of other races? What sort of transformation is happening in these penal colonies to turn the convict into colonial lord? The French government in particular was concerned with this puzzle, as evidenced by the debates that were spurred by administrative reports from New Caledonia: was life too hard or too easy for the convicts? Should they be treated as prisoners or settlers? Stephen Toth has argued that the ideological incoherence of the practices of penal colonization led to the French cessation of the practice in the late nineteenth century.[29]

The self-examination and vulnerability to criticism that result from practices of punishment and colonization are similar: in the name of what ideal do we engage in this practice? The transition from one regime to the next brings the opportunity for new consciousness of political order, a theme captured by Kafka's description of the passing of the order from the old Commandant to the new Commandant. In a sense, we are all outsiders with an ability to see events and practices without a dulled consciousness at the beginning of a new regime. Colonization also creates the conditions that juxtapose outside perspective onto the common assumptions and practices of all cultures involved. Conquest in the name of civilization is a difficult proposition to maintain, as is administration of pain in the name of enlightenment—particularly before an audience. It is abundantly clear in Kafka's short story "Jackals and Arabs" that he was aware of the difficult relationship between the triad of European values and dignitaries from home, the conduct of colonial settlers who presumably reflect those same values, and the natives.[30]

Kafka's machine in the colony speaks to all of these dynamics: the potentially catalyzing spectacle of punishment, the arrival of "civilization" in the colonies, and the political opportunities and risks afforded by the audience. The result shocks us into a new consciousness about the claims of enlightenment and the political administrations under its banner. The elements of the machine perfectly embody the qualities of European civilization: its mechanisms adapt to different bodies to serve justice equally well to all; it is transparent and impartial, and denies the ability to seek revenge by those in power by taking the ability to punish and putting it in nonhuman hands. And, as I have already noted, it realizes the sentence with perfect efficiency and mimesis: the sentence, no more no less, *is* the punishment. Our own mechanisms of justice only aspire to such dispassionate administration and such clear effect.[31]

In a fashion typical of Kafka, he neatly subverts all of our expectations and standard narratives about progress. The passing of the regime from the old Commandant, one based on faith, into the realm of the new Commandant is quickly assumed to be progressive as the machine has fallen into disfavor. But the faith of the old Commandant was not religious, it was earthly: he had faith in engineering and human understanding. The typical colonial narrative is also reversed—rather than finding the settlers have "gone native," the explorer finds that the most vehement advocates of the principles of the homeland are in the periphery. The explorer ultimately refuses to condemn the machine publicly and to adopt the task of redeeming those hidden away in the penal colony. The characters in the story are so disorienting to the reader that Kafka leaves the machine as the only fixed point: we realize with horror that the Harrow is more civilized than the population it was created to enlighten. But such a position is untenable: how can a torture device reflect the values of humanism in any scenario?

We don't like the machine, particularly since it amplifies our desire for the engineering of perfect justice to such effect. But we are left with the feeling that the penal colony won't necessarily be a better place without it. The machine stands for the hope of earthly redemption before death—at any price. Denied any easy answers to the predicaments of the penal colony, the explorer leaves. And so today, denied any easy answers about what exactly is achieved in punishment and whether it truly embodies our social values, we chose to turn away as well. Why go out of the way to view what is hidden? Punishment was once a public affair; citizens even visited penitentiaries to view the scales of justice at work. Today executions, incarceration, censorship are all topics of public debate, but the actual administration of punishment is something that we would prefer not to see.

What we need to carry away from Kafka's story is how impossible it is to find solid ground in terms of punishment and its purpose, idealism, and practice. However, the absence of secure footing in the negotiation between relinquishing and pursuing ideals does not change the fact that being an audience or witness nonetheless changes the dynamics of punishment and its relationship to justice. But this is one of the more intractable problems of political regimes, that their accountability rests upon the willingness of others to witness the execution of its ideals. Those who have the choice to leave or ignore state punishment rarely persist in this responsibility. Those who are forced to feel or administer the law lack the perspective and moral authority of an audience.

CHAPTER 2

"Man's Life Is but a Prison"

Human Reason, Secular Political Order, and the Punishments of God

Race of Cain, ascend to heaven,
And cast God down upon the earth.
—Charles Baudelaire, *Flowers of Evil*

Punishment is a reflection of political order in all of its complexity. It requires an active relationship between justice and power, a negotiation of perception between government and population, and finally, a reckoning of the relationship between political ideals and practical administration. My description of political order is deliberately participatory. This presents the question of why a given population would want to create a power to punish itself. Without a satisfactory explanation of this phenomenon, my conjecture—that punishment is not simply about demonstrating the power of command over a population as much as expressing an authority that originates from this population—crumbles. The answer to this question can be found in the Bible, and in Hobbes's *Leviathan* that reveals how the foundations of political order moved from the heavens to the earth.

This chapter explores the connections between human reason, punishment, and political order by looking at Hobbes's *Leviathan* as a response to Job's pleas for comprehension of human suffering in the book of Job. *Leviathan* offers punishment and a political order that is transparent to human reason; after all, a political order we cannot understand does not allow us to exercise our judgment and control our destiny. Viewing the two works in conjunction reveals how Hobbes offers a corrective to Christianity's failure to provide clear causality.

One of Hobbes's greatest insights was that the anxiety resulting from our desire to control our future, combined with our inability to do so, finds expression in political ordering. Systems of punishment are one of the primary mechanisms of political order that address our need for causality and the anxiety that accompanies it. The impulse to order amidst chaos has led us to construct ever more refined systems of creating predictability. Punishment follows the system of logic by replacing the unexpectedness of criminality or violence with the predictability of pain following an ill deed. Punishment and political order reflect the human mind interacting with and interpreting the phenomenal world; perceiving this contingent relationship helps us to understand the very root of secular political systems.

The Demand for Punishment

Contemporary readers encountering Hobbes for the first time find it almost impossible to imagine *Leviathan* as an attractive political vision. Why would anyone embrace an all-powerful ruler? The short answer to this question lies in the Hobbesian vision of the state of nature that reflects the turmoil of his time: his philosophy was born from the same fear he claimed as his twin. As Corey Robin's recent examination of Hobbes explicates, fear is the foundational political psychology of liberalism—a tendency that is particularly relevant in times of turmoil and change. Fears of the unknown and unknowable can be transformed through political order to a more calculable, and ultimately productive, fear of worldly authority. Punishment is assumed to be a primary instrument of this regime since it allows the sovereign to realize the threat of pain, and hence manipulate and transform individual fear into collective harmony. The central understanding of the relationship between punishment and politics is that punishment displays the power of command and establishes and maintains hierarchical authority. The Leviathan punishes in order to transform our fear of one another into fear of the potentially avoidable fury of the sovereign.

Nietzsche considerably complicates this picture in *On the Genealogy of Morals* by asserting that punishment is a power of the community recently stolen by the state in its quest for dominance. The origins of punishment lie in the community's desire to extract payment from those who abuse their membership or take it for granted—for example, the thief who steals from his neighbor's pot will be reminded of the protection afforded by the village once he is ejected into the woods. Nietzsche's observation that "in punishment there is so much that is festive!" has disturbed many readers in arguing that punishment serves as the basis for, not merely the right of, the community.[1] The origins of the social contract lie not in the reasoned calculations of individuals, but rather in festivals of suffering that affirm membership in the collective.

But perhaps the two versions of punishment are not so far apart after all. In Hobbes, the community creates a demi-God and awards him the power to punish—what was originally an expression and experience of the community becomes condensed into the figure of the "Artificiall Man." But in the end, the function of punishment is the same: to demonstrate the power of either the community or its representative and to enforce compliance with a given political order. Punishment generates and manipulates fear. However, this view of punishment is unidirectional: it affirms a view of political authority based upon hierarchical relationships. What this vision lacks is an understanding of why we might seek punishment, and why we would welcome the administration of pain. This is not a case for popular masochism of gigantic proportions, the counterpart to Nietzsche's intonations of collective sadism. Instead Hobbes offers an understanding of how not just fear but also hope and the proclivities of human rationality lead us to the construction of an all-powerful entity to deliver punishment. Our craving for comprehensible order, not discipline, is what inspired the creation of an earthly deity to punish and hence redeem us.

Fear may govern the direction of Leviathan, but Hobbes also examines the psychological drive of humans in another sense. He asserts that causality is the primary tool used by humans to assert control over their lives and environments, rather than being subject to them in the way of other creatures. If something happens, we want to know why. Determining the cause of events allows us to prevent tragedy, or attempt to re-create or to perpetuate fortune. This human proclivity forms the starting point of Hobbes's political vision in *Leviathan*. He eloquently states that "it is peculiar to the nature of men to be inquisitive into the causes of the events they see—some more, some less, but all men so much as to be curious in the search of the causes of their own good and evil fortune."[2] This inclination toward causality propels the establishment and perpetuation of political order to help guarantee the expected order of events. The promise of political order is that everything will progress in a relatively predictable manner—justice and virtue shall be rewarded, indolence punished. Even more mundanely, political order offers the hope that everyday life will be more calculable despite the intrusion of unfortunate events: you can put funds in a bank that will be guaranteed even if the bank is robbed; if a house catches fire you can call the fire department and someone will respond.

But while this proclivity toward causality has been at the root of all political orders, it is a necessarily tragic propensity. Causal logic offers the tantalizing possibility that we can know why things occur and, even more important, that we might be able to control what happens to us. However, experience proves that a complete mastery of events is impossible. For example, routine maintenance does not always preclude automobile failure, and reward does not inevitably follow accomplishment. Our perpetually unsuccessful attempts to control our lives and fortunes are shadowed by a nagging unease. The frequently suppressed knowledge that absolute control cannot be maintained creates the psychology of anxiety common in human beings. We set the stage to create calm and clear progression yet know that our narrative is bound to be disrupted in ways we cannot anticipate. The inevitable failure spurs us on to try to create ever more tight contingency plans, which unfailingly fall short as well.

The search for causality is the source of anxiety, but it also can provide comfort when our plans go awry and we suffer. We can look back and see different choices or paths that might be taken, or we can comfort ourselves with the knowledge that there will be some reward for the pain we feel currently. Punishment isn't just about Nietzsche's relation between creditor and debtor, but also about the relationship between God and man. We might suffer today, but that pain will lead to redemption. *Leviathan* and the book of Job help us to understand why we would be inclined to view suffering as punishment, or even welcome punishment as a path to redemption. Hobbes's Leviathan delivers punishment that enforces order based upon human reason. But it simultaneously reveals the Achilles' heel of any secular regime: the requirement that punishment provide earthly redemption.

The Fall from Grace: How Judgment Begat Punishment

In the Christian tradition, the ability to judge gives birth to the punishments of God. Before they are able to know the difference between right and wrong, Adam and Eve have not been punished, they dwell in Paradise and have been given life everlasting. God tells Adam, the day he eats the fruit from the tree of the knowledge of good and evil he shall die. Adam and Eve eat the fruit and do not die. The fruit itself does not kill them; instead mortality becomes their punishment for disobeying God. The punishment for the crime brings on their eventual death. After Adam and Eve gain the faculty of judgment through their disobedience God observes, "Behold, the man has become like one of us, knowing good and evil; and now lest he put forth his hand and take also the tree of life, and eat, and live forever" (Genesis 4:22). God doesn't conclude his thought, that then humans will have become Gods, knowing and immortal. Instead, he banishes humans from Paradise, cursing them to suffer estrangement and pain, and to return to dust at the end of their lives.

The story is important primarily because it offers an explanation for the suffering that humans endure. We humans brought the state of original sin upon ourselves, hence our state of life is one long punishment from God. Consider the link between the faculty of judgment and the punishment that is wrought as a result. The punishment of God would not have made sense without the faculty gained by the crime. Dying from eating the fruit would have been a causal relation that any animal would have been able to learn from. This fruit is poisonous. But to understand that disobedience itself is wicked, not merely the consequence of disobedience, relies upon the faculty of judgment. A child can disobey her father and touch a hot stove, and will learn why not to touch a hot stove out of instinct and experience. To teach a child not to disobey even when there are no direct consequences for his or her actions is a much more difficult enterprise. Why is lying wrong if no one finds out? Understanding this requires a faculty of judgment, the ability to know the difference between good and evil as abstract principles.

In punishing Adam and Eve, God not only dooms them to lives of pain, but also takes the first step in developing their ill-gotten faculty of judgment. The story is intended to provide a causal answer to the suffering of humanity. Humans suffer because Adam and Eve sinned, and through punishment humans will learn to remember and act correctly when judgment is required.

However, there is another way to understand this story. Faced with suffering, our desire for order requires us to understand the human condition as punishment based upon a clear order—God's will. If we suffer, there must be a reason that we do so; it cannot be senseless and random. To understand our suffering *as punishment* comes from the faculty of judgment. The faculty of judgment leads us to assume that there must be a cause and effect between our actions and lives.

There is a remarkable convergence of the two interpretations here. In the first, sin creates punishment. Yet we can also see that the content of the sin is not inconsequential—judgment creates the proclivity to see suffering as punishment. We insist that the random chaos of life and death is the result of a divine order of reward and penalty. Human reason creates this order out of faith; though life and death appear random, they are ordered by a force we cannot see or understand. The insistence that such chaos is ordered, despite the dearth of empirical evidence that proves this order, demonstrates the fervent human desire for causality and control.

The Book of Job

Divine punishment and original sin help our minds make sense of suffering. Inherent in our desire to understand punishment is the potential for future control, not just explanation of past events. This was true for the Greeks for whom punishing was a form of honor—a reciprocal relationship. We punish in the hope that we will achieve a better world, make better judgments next time. Therefore, the conception of original sin defies our conception of punishment. If we were born evil, if we will be punished no matter what, then what is the use of trying to be good? Why would God issue the Ten Commandments if we were to be punished whether or not we followed them?

Further reading of the Old Testament reveals a more complex view of the nature of divine punishment, most pointedly and powerfully displayed in *The Book of Job*.[3] Here the human hope that through obedience we can avoid divine punishment is reconciled with the reality of random suffering. Man's capacity for judgment is more clearly defined. Interestingly, there is a shift from the observations of God and the serpent in Genesis who hinted that the capacity of Adam and Eve to know good and evil makes them like God, implying that divine and human moral reasoning are equivalent. In *The Book of Job*, human rationality is defined as distinctly different from the rationale that guides the bestowal of divine rewards and penalties.

The Book of Job opens with a description of the grace bestowed upon Job's life by God. He has three beautiful daughters and seven strong sons, and was "the richest man in the East." Job was a "man of perfect integrity, who feared God and avoided evil" (5). Job follows God's rules and reaps the rewards of God's favor. Nonetheless, every year after a week of celebration Job would have his children be purified, "for he thought, 'Perhaps my children have sinned, and cursed God in their hearts'" (5). Here the fundamental uncertainty of man's ability to avoid divine punishment is revealed. Job opens his house to every stranger and humbly thanks God every day, yet the fear that somehow, somewhere, something could go terribly wrong haunts him in the midst of his plenty. The hope that the devout can avoid punishment is shadowed by the fear that punishment will come nonetheless, no matter how strident their efforts. After all, it was clear that sometimes innocents suffered, while those who were less than devout were rewarded by fate. *The Book of Job* acknowledges that divine order is still unexpected: even divine punishment can be random.

An Accusing Angel appears before God and responds when God boasts of the integrity and piety of Job, "Doesn't Job have a good reason for being so good? Haven't you put a hedge around him—himself and his whole family and everything he has? You bless whatever he does, and the land is teeming with his cattle. But just reach out and strike everything he has, and I bet he'll curse you to your face" (6). God gives leave to the Angel to test Job's faith. The Angel takes all his possessions and kills his family. Job still will not curse God, so the Angel sends him boils that eat away at his flesh and cause excruciating pain. After one week, Job cries, "God damn the day I was born and the night that forced me from the womb" (13). He begs for death and proclaims the injustice of God's order.

If God is all-powerful, why do the innocent suffer, and why does evil go unpunished? How can we explain the misfortune of the devout when those who flout God's laws enjoy life? The suffering of Job calls attention to the inconsistencies of God's punishments and demands an accounting. The rest of the book is Job's dialogue with his three friends and then God himself about the nature of divine punishment. Job insists that he is innocent, that God punishes him without reason and is therefore unjust. His friends beg him to be humble and proclaim his sins and beg for forgiveness. Eliphaz asks rhetorically, "Can an innocent man be punished?" assuming that the answer is no. Yet *The Book of Job* leaves the question open, for the story itself suggests the opposite answer. Eliphaz insists that man could never avoid being wicked. Job retorts, "Can't I tell right from wrong? If I sinned, wouldn't I know it?"

(22). Job's friends turn to faith and the answer of original sin to explain his suffering, Job relies upon his judgment to affirm his devoutness. He points out the misery of human existence: "Man's life is a prison; he is sentenced to pain and grief" (23). Is life itself nothing but a punishment by a vindictive God? Is divine punishment inescapable?

Job refuses to succumb to the pleading of his friends. He insists upon his innocence, proclaiming the injustice of God.

> I swear by God, who has wronged me
> And filled my cup with despair,
> That while there is life in this body
> And as long as I can breathe,
> I will never let you convict me;
> I will never give up my claim.
> I will hold tight to my innocence;
> My mind will never submit. (64)

Job knows he is innocent. Because God punishes the innocent, he is unjust.[4]

God comes to earth and speaks to Job and his friends from a whirlwind and immediately complicates the situation by asking, "Do you dare to deny my judgment? Am I wrong because you are right?" (84). The simple binary of guilt and innocence is swept away. The human capacity to see punishment and reward as proof of either guilt or innocence is entirely too clumsy an attempt at justice. God's reason works in ways that are truly unfathomable to the human mind. While the suffering of the meek and reward of the venal may appear as injustice to us, this is a failure of our comprehension, not of divine justice. The voice in the whirlwind taunts Job and says he could punish all the proud and humiliate all the wicked, but this would not be divine rule; he calls it "savage justice."

Job is converted; he acknowledges the limits of his reason. "I will be quiet, comforted that I am dust," he concludes. Therefore the contradictory becomes reconciled. Job was innocent, but God is just. There is a fundamental inability of human rationality to understand the order created by God's punishments. We can strive to follow his rules and use our judgment in ways that he would find praiseworthy, but this does not mean we shall not suffer at his hand someday. The crushing reality of punishment has outstripped our attempts to rationally order cause and effect. Job was right to fear that suffering would invade his life, even when he had done everything possible to curry God's favor.

After Job's realization of the impenetrable logic of divine punishment, *The Book of Job* ends with one last Psalm. God rewards Job and punishes his friends. Job has "spoken the truth about me," while the friends with all their piety failed to do the same. Job understands the limits of his reason, that God punishes the innocent, and that the order of the world is beyond his grasp. The friends are punished because they assume they know the mind of God; they assumed that the source of Job's suffering rested in his actions. In other words, it is a sin to expect God's actions to conform to human reason. Divine order is beyond our conceptual grasp.

Job's Trial

One of the more curious elements in *The Book of Job* is a pretend trial that is constructed by Job and his friends. His friends urge him to plead his case before God, confess his sins and beg for mercy. This leads Job to contemplate such a trial and make a number of observations. First, if God is the judge and prosecutor and Job is the defendant, the grounds of their collision are entirely uneven. "I know that this is true: no man can argue with God or answer even one of a thousand accusations. However wise or powerful—who could oppose him and live?" (27). There is no way to state a case before a creature so much more powerful than oneself. The lack of even proximate equality makes an interchange impossible. To hold a trial between unequals is preposterous.

Second, Job asks, "If he seized me, who could stop him or cry out, 'What are you doing?'" (27). There must be someone even more powerful who could make sure that the trial proceeded fairly. Why should he appear in court if there is no guarantee of his safety? How could he freely accuse him without the protection of a greater individual? Job ponders: "If only there were an arbiter who could lay his hand on us both, who could make you put down your club and hold back your terrible arm. Then without fear, I would say, You have not treated me justly" (29). The judge in a case must be neutral, and more powerful than the participants; otherwise a fair hearing cannot be achieved.

Finally, Job expresses his desire that the punishment he has endured be redemptive. Even if it has proven to be unjust, he would be willing to endure it if it meant that God would embrace him for doing so.

If only you would hide me in the pit
Till your anger has passed away,
Then come to me and release me.
All my days in prison
I would sit and wait for that time.
You would call me—I would answer;
You would come to me and rejoice,
Delighting in my smallest step
Like a father watching his child. (37)

This is a crucial revelation. Job welcomes God's authority, even the administration of punishment, as long as it leads to redemption. He is willing to endure hardship for the sake of God's authority, as long as he is congratulated for doing so. If he felt that the punishment has redeemed him in God's eyes, the bond between punisher and punished would only be strengthened. This shows the inexorable desire of human rationality to ascribe cause and effect. God has denied Job the understanding of a causal link between crime and punishment in this case. Indeed, there was no causal relationship to understand. Even if there was no crime that brought on punishment, if the punishment yields redemption a causal relation is established. Job can accept his punishment—even if he can't understand why he is being punished— as long as the punishment leads to redemption.

Job's attempt to reason about the conditions of just punishment and to ascribe meaning to his travails is answered by God in the form of a great sea creature—Leviathan. He describes a most terrible, irascible monster that no human could even dare to imagine placating. Only God has the power to subdue him. Job accepts this illustration of divine might and human impotence. The question of justice seems to have been solved by the assertion of supreme power. God is all-powerful; therefore you cannot question his justice.

Leviathan Returns

Thomas Hobbes adopted the name of this sea creature, Leviathan, for his artificial and all-powerful earthly God. A number of scholars have observed that Hobbes carried the lesson of the sea monster away from the book of Job—might makes right. If the sea monster can be used to frighten Job into accepting God's impenetrable divine judgment, why could it not work to reinforce mortal authorities as well? While the family resemblance is certainly there, the connections between Job and Hobbes are more complex than that. Hobbes not only adopts God's method of affirming his right to judge, he responds to Job's pleas during his trial earlier in the text as well.

Clearly Hobbes was closely engaged in a reading of the Bible. Recent scholarship has exhaustively debated whether Hobbes was truly devout. There are those who say that he was devout[5] and those that argue he was not.[6] Remarkably, none of these commentators looks very closely at the relationship between Hobbes's *Leviathan* and the source of its central concept, the book of Job. Deborah Baumgold does broach the subject, asserting, "Figuratively, the political theory is about leviathan and behemoth, but it speaks to Job."[7] Yet Baumgold asserts this in the most general fashion, believing that Hobbes was interested not only in the powerful of the world, but also in providing for the powerless. W. H. Greenleaf has established through careful historical research that Hobbes was reading contemporary commentaries on the book of Job by J. Caryl.[8] Greenleaf argues that there are parallels in the political implications of Job's story and Hobbes's *Leviathan*, but his main goal in this note is to place the ideas of Hobbes within the context of debates about theological nominalism.[9] I am not trying to argue that the linkage between Hobbes and the book of Job reveals something in particular about Hobbes's relationship to Christianity. Instead, the connections between the two works help to illuminate Hobbes's project in a new light, as well as establish how conceptions of punishment reveal a shifting role in the relationship between human rationality and political order.

One interpretation of the book of Job's resolution is that the monster makes divine and human reason expendable: justice is based only on power. In an influential article from 1983, R. J. Halliday, Timothy Kenyon, and Andrew Reeve claimed, "For Hobbes, the lesson of Job contained an important political message: the absolutism of the mortal God is an imitation of the irresistible power of the immortal God. And obviously, Hobbes was quite content to rest on this doctrine."[10] I disagree with this assertion. First of all, Hobbes does more than adopt the monster from the book of Job; there is a clear intertextuality between Job's trial and Hobbes's *Leviathan* that suggests Hobbes carried away much more than this basic political message. Second, while Hobbes may have embraced the relationship between power and justice demonstrated in the book of Job, he also makes an important distinction between his Leviathan and the self-declaredly opaque God that resisted Job's logic. The absolutism of the immortal God of Job includes a statement that his actions are inscrutable to humans. Hobbes empathizes with Job's predicament and creates a Leviathan that can be understood by human—in fact, he only exists through the perception and reason of human beings.

Michael Oakeshott has argued that while Hobbes's work may appear labyrinthine, it is connected together by one thread—the nature of human reason.

> It is the character of reasoning that determines the range and the limits of philosophical enquiry; it is this character that gives coherence, system, to Hobbes's philosophy. Philosophy, for him, is the world as it appears in the mirror of reason; civil philosophy is the image of civil order reflected in that mirror. In general, the world seen in this mirror is a world of causes and effects; cause and effect are its categories. And for Hobbes reason has two alternative ends; to determine the conditional causes of given effects, or to determine the conditional effects of given causes.[11]

Placing Hobbes's interest in cause and effect as the primary categories of human reason at the center of analysis, we can see why Hobbes found a kindred spirit in the figure of Job. Job's meticulous worship of God in the face of his prosperity sought to affirm devotion and reward. His fear of the unknown or the unexpected, causing him to purify his children year after year just in case they had thought something that might displease God, reveals what Hobbes called the fundamental human anxiety—the desire to know and the fear of the unknowable.

In chapter 12, "Of Religion," Hobbes argues that the origins of religion can be found in the psyche of man. The primary disposition of human beings is to seek the causes of events that they see, then to establish cause and effect between chains of events. The problem is that causality is usually obscure. "And when he cannot assure himselfe of the true causes of things, (for the causes of good and evill fortune for the most part are invisible,) he supposes causes of them, either such as his own fancy suggesteth; or trusteth to the Authority of other men, such as he thinks to be his friends, and wiser than himself."[12] The need to find causality overcomes the lack of empirical evidence. When there is no clear cause of an event, we will assume one anyway. Hobbes believes this is the impetus behind the development of religion as an unseen force that can explain why events occur as they do.

Yet the search for causality combined with the impossibility of perceiving the cause of many occurrences leads to acute anxiety. Particularly those who meticulously try to anticipate the future and provide for themselves become haunted by the capriciousness of fate. "So that man, which looks too far before him, in the care of future time, hath his heart all the day long, gnawed on by fear of death, poverty, or other calamity; and has no repose, nor pause of his anxiety, but in sleep" (76). While it is certainly debatable whether such anxiety is indeed overcome by sleep, the image is startlingly clear. The more one tries to control one's destiny, the more anxious one becomes in recognizing that many aspects of the world are out of control. Here Job's furtive prayers and purification rites, just in case his children had sinned somehow, spring to mind. When Job's punishment is wrought, he cries out, "My worst fears have happened; My nightmares have come to life."[13]

Hobbes describes how religion works to provide a clear causality for events that cannot be otherwise explained. The propensity to assert such a train of events even when events defy explanation is remarkable. Hobbes notes, "And therefore, men by their own meditation, arrive to the acknowledgement of one Infinite, Omnipotent, and Eternall God, choose rather to confesse he is Incomprehensible, and above their understanding; than to define his Nature by Spirit Incorporeall, and then confesse their definition to be unintelligible" (77). The mind that creates phantoms and other bodies to ease the anxiety of uncertainty will not relinquish these solutions even when they fail to provide any explanatory satisfaction. Here Hobbes is unquestionably referring to Job, where God's majesty is accepted as beyond human understanding. This is a crucial paradox to explore: the mind's need for causality is so great that it would rather blame its own limitations than give up the device that provides a sense of causality. But while ultimately Job appears to put his mind at rest with a knowledge of limited understanding and be "comforted that he is dust," the entire story of Job reveals a more indeterminate struggle between the need for rational explanation and the opacity of divine punishment. Job continues to want punishment to be perceptible to his reason, to have a clear cause and effect. Perhaps the impulse of reason proves triumphant over the need to assert causality. This seems to be where Hobbes offers the answer to Job's dilemma. Hobbes will invent a creature that punishes, but it will be carefully subject to the logic of human rationality, while at the same time embodying the superhuman power of the divine.

Hobbes's ruler may bring terrible punishments to bear upon its subjects, but these punishments will meet the criteria outlined by Job. They will be subject to the categories of cause and effect, there will be a powerful judge to arbitrate, and the subjects shall be equal before the law. In short, punishment will be rational, hence redemptive when administered, and possible to predict, comprehend, and hence potentially avoid. The book of Job offered an explanation for the breakdown of causality between piety and divine grace.

But Job's cries ultimately did not go unheeded. *Leviathan* can be read as an attempt to answer Job's pleas, to create a political order that is based upon awesome power yet not opaque to human reason. Even if divine order cannot be made accountable to human reason and control, the worldly order can become so. Hobbes marks a shift in the relationship between human reason and the creation of systems of punishment. If human reason invented original sin to make sense of suffering, this is the next step along the way. Reason will not only be able to explain punishment but will also be able to predict and thereby respond to it. Punishment can be truly redemptive if it meets these conditions. A system of punishment that follows the logic of human reason promises a more transparent ordering of the world and the powers within it.

Hobbes's Theory of Punishment

Punishment plays a most central yet generally unexamined aspect in the political philosophy of Thomas Hobbes. But to understand his system of punishment, it is necessary to situate it in the context of his epistemology, which has been thoroughly explored by scholars. Hobbes states that all thoughts and imagination originate from the senses. He begins his book with the chapter "On Sense" highlighting this element as the basis of his political order. Sense provides the origin of our perception of the world, "(For there is no conception in a mans mind, which hath not at first, totally, or by parts, been begotten upon the organs of sense.)" (13). The senses do not provide us access to what is per se; but are only "a Representation or Appearance" (13). Hobbes does not thereby conclude that we should suspend judgment, since we cannot know whether our perceptions of reality are true or not, as is the case with skepticism. Richard Tuck has traced links between Hobbes's interest in perception and knowledge and the work of Descartes, Mersenne, and Gassendi in developing a postskeptical approach.[14] These seventeenth-century thinkers seem to have drawn inspiration from Epicurus, "who was recorded as having said something to the effect that 'every phantasia is true.'"[15] Recent research also suggests that Hobbes's exposure to optical instruments while living in exile in Paris played a more formative role in the development of his political philosophy than previously understood.[16] Regardless, Hobbes saw human knowledge as based upon external stimulation of the senses, despite the fact that our perception was not necessarily representational. He points out that our dreams are affected by the external circumstances of our sleeping (for example, "lying cold breedeth dreams of fear"). Through the senses, external reality influences perception. He is not breaking off into a radically self-constructed system of knowledge. But nonetheless, perception, not empiricism, forms the basis of knowledge. Hence, any social and political order must be based upon our perceptions. The weakness of Christian order is that it relies too much on elements, such as divine justice, that are explicitly beyond human perceptual faculties.

The body receives the senses, and the mind sets about ordering them. Senses provide the material for rationality to exercise itself by developing a "trayne of imaginations." These are the categories of cause and effect; our senses inform us, for example, that when it rains a particular road floods, and the next time it rains we can imagine that the same road has flooded. In that way, sense meets the human inclination to establish cause and effect. The result is science, which Hobbes defines as follows.

> Science is the knowledge of Consequences, and dependence of one fact upon another; by which, out of that we can presently do, we know how to do something else when we will, or the like, another time: Because when we see how any thing comes about, upon what causes, and by what manner; when the like causes come into our power, we see how to make it produce the like effects. (35–36)

Science allows us to learn from the past and try to exert control over the future, to anticipate and plan.

Hobbes developed his metaphors carefully, and therefore I do not take lightly the fact that he described punishment as the "nerves of the Artificiall Man, the Common-wealth." The relationship between nerves and action is mechanical. If you hit your thumb with a hammer, the hand will recoil and blood will rush into the appendage automatically. The sensation of pain will be registered in the mind, which will then direct the body to be more careful next time. Punishment and reward are the nerves of the commonwealth, "by which fastned to the seate of the Soveraignty, every joynt and member is moved to performe his duty" (9). If someone steals from another, the brain (sovereign) of the commonwealth responds and causes pain to the criminal. The sensation will teach him, and all who watch, the cause and effect of disturbing the order. Similarly, those who protect the commonwealth will be rewarded, teaching through sensation the cause and effect of pleasure.

Once again, the matter is one of perception. As Hobbes observes, the purpose of punishment is not revenge but correction. Therefore the sovereign needs to punish in ways that correct rather than cultivate resentment. If crimes are committed out of fear, need, or ignorance "there is place many times for Lenity" (241). On the other hand, crimes committed by the privileged need to be punished fervently. "For indignation carrieth men, not onely against the Actors, and Authors of injustice; but against all Power that is likely to protect them" (241). If the body of the commonwealth perceives that punishment is driven by something other than the performance of justice, the nerves of the body will no longer achieve its goal of training its appendages. If through punishment the commonwealth betrays favoritism or prejudice, the body will respond to those sensations instead.

The causal relationship Hobbes is searching for here is not a direct correspondence between punishment and crime. If this were the case, theft would be punished in the same way, regardless of who committed it and why. Rather, humans need to be able to *perceive* a direct correspondence between crime and punishment. Therefore, punishment needs to occur as a clear message to the members of the commonwealth. It is with this goal in mind that Hobbes elaborates the rules and methods of punishment in chapter 28, "Of Punishments and Rewards." In contrast to the trials of Job, Hobbesian punishment must be perfectly transparent lest it lose its utility.

Nor is it simply the sovereign's ability to punish that informs the body. If Hobbes were adopting a simple linkage between power and might, then the mere ability of the sovereign to punish, and punish terribly, would be considered sufficient to generate adherence to the law. Yet Hobbes quite specifically delineates how the sovereign should punish. Because punishments and rewards send particular lessons and teach the body through sensation it is important that the sovereign punish and reward correctly in order to teach the body the correct response.

Hobbes details the conditions of just punishment in chapter 28: "A Punishment, is an Evill inflicted by publique Authority, on him that hath done, or omitted that which is Judged by the same Authority to be a Transgression of the Law: to the end that the will of men may thereby the better be disposed to obedience" (214). There are several aspects of this definition to be elaborated. First, the actions of private men are not included in his definition. Only those with public authority can punish. Those who are sworn enemies of the public authority are also not subject to punishment, either because they were never subject to the law or have declared themselves no longer subject to the law. The pain that a power may inflict upon those outside the law is pure hostility instead of punishment. Hobbes also distinguishes divine punishment, misfortune such as plague or illness that befalls someone after a transgression of divine law, from human variants. The result of these qualifications is that punishment is a product of the social contract and hence also a product of human perception and reason. This means that noncitizens and an opponent facing a conquered enemy are not subject to the same restrictions that Hobbes places upon the public authority.

Some argue that the sovereign authority's power makes the law; the law is created and maintained by his authority to punish those who transgress it. But the second notable aspect of Hobbes's description of punishment is that he carefully limits the sovereign power's ability to punish. Here the mere fact of punishment does not establish sovereignty, instead sovereignty bounds the ability to punish. In a fashion all the more remarkable considering his leniency toward the necessities of sovereign power at other locations in the text, Hobbes places a series of restrictions upon punishment. Hobbes's standards of punishment are surprisingly rigid—it must be rational, redemptive, and transparent— all the elements that Job desires for his own trial.

Only through the perception of causality between crime and punishment, and then punishment and redemption, does punishment become useful in training members of the commonwealth. For that reason, "all evill which is inflicted without intention or possibility of disposing the

Delinqquent, or (by his example) other men, to obeey the Lawes, is not Punishment; but an act of hostility" (215). Punishment is distinguished from hostility only by its utility. Furthermore, he elaborates that punishment must follow public condemnation and announcement of exactly which crime or crimes are being punished.

In achieving the perceptible relationship between the punishment and just authority, Hobbes makes the following provisions. First, the amount of punishment needs to be exact in order to achieve its utility. The pain of punishment must outweigh the benefits derived from the crime, otherwise it will not create adherence to the law. More interesting, Hobbes also states that if a punishment for a crime has been specified, increasing the penalty is not legitimate punishment but is instead "an act of hostility." This provision belies the assumption that for Hobbes might makes right. Instead, punishment must adhere to the law in order to generate obedience to the law. Furthermore, a person cannot be punished for breaking a law that does not exist.

The public authority alone has the right to punish. Hobbes distinguishes punishment from private acts of revenge, as well as acts of nature or God, such as a curse or illness that fall upon someone after they have done evil (214–15). This makes it seem as though one aspect of the generation of sovereignty is the exclusive ability to punish. Yet Hobbes points out that wanton punishment by the sovereign, which may assert his power, nonetheless defeats the enterprise of punishment, which is to generate judgment and obedience. If punishment breaks a person's spirit, or strikes fear and terror in the hearts of spectators, fear is the result, not the improvement of judgment. In order to train the judgment of members of the commonwealth, the relationship between law, authority, and the punishment must be maintained as well.

This is yet another way that Hobbes answers Job's pleas for a redemptive punishment. Hobbes places the conditions of punishment under a utilitarian imperative: if it is not useful for bolstering the judgment of the commonwealth, it should not be done. For this reason, "All Punishments of Innocent subjects, be they great or little, are against the Law of Nature: For Punishment is only for transgression of the Law, and therefore there can be no Punishment of the Innocent. . . . For there can arrive no good to the Common-wealth, by punishing the innocent" (219). It is not the mere exercise of power that guarantees the obedience of subjects, it is the exercise of power in ways that both conform to causal logic and are perceptible to human reason that help form the "nerves" of the polity. Only through the consistent application of causality in both crime and punishment, and a demonstrably clear relationship between legal authority and punishment, can the Hobbesian order be maintained.

Conclusion

Hobbes's *Leviathan* and *The Book of Job* offer us one way to evaluate our political order: does it meet the demands of causality, and is the justice meted out perceptible as such? Looking at the contemporary penal system in the United States, it must be admitted that it meets neither of these criteria. The links between crime and punishment, and between punishment and redemption, have been severed. Those in prison often feel that their incarceration was random, therefore unjust. Dozens of people engage in similar criminal activities yet are not caught and sentenced. The perception of irregularity extends into white-collar crime as well; for example, ask other people whether they think insider trading is consistently punished. Nor does having undergone punishment lead to redemption. Megan's Law provides for the permanent stigmatization of some offenders; employment and suffrage exclusions create a multitiered system of full and partial citizenship. All of these problems have been noted by others as unjust for those unfortunate enough to be subject to them. This reading suggests why these practices may be detrimental to our entire political order.

The other lesson that emerges here is what Hobbes establishes about the desire for control when confronted with a chaotic world that drives us to establish, revise, and insist upon political order. This also seems to be a lesson that is worth heeding in the contemporary political climate. People certainly do look to their government to eradicate the unforeseeable and mitigate misfortune. It will inevitably fail in its attempts to accomplish these tasks.

Perhaps the true dynamism of political systems is the paradox that gave birth to them: the human desire to order the universe and find stability combined with the persistence of the unforeseeable. Embedded in human reason is the anxiety that will drive us to find different, more responsive orders. This is a search that will never end, unless we one day decide to liberate ourselves from the prison of our anxiety and hence overcome the need for political order. The most prescient example of this sort of transcendence is found in Camus' "Myth of Sisyphus." Instead of trying to eliminate suffering by creating systems of order based upon human reason, Camus suggests that we will finally end our suffering by realizing that it has no meaning. Perhaps the attempt to see meaning in our suffering is the source of suffering.

In Camus' essay, Sisyphus pushes the rock up the hill and wearily treads back after it rolls down again, doomed to meaningless labor for eternity. Camus perversely suggests that he holds out the key to our happiness. When Sisyphus turns back to descend the hill toward his rock, how does he face the external futility of his efforts? "If this myth is tragic, that is because his hero is conscious. Where would his torture be, indeed, if at every step the hope of succeeding upheld him?"[17] Sisyphus's punishment of rolling the rock for eternity is inconceivable since he knows the absolute futility of his actions. Camus suggests he becomes free through being denied redemption in his punishment, by knowing that his efforts will lead him nowhere but back to the beginning. He is set free by knowing that he has created his destiny, yet it is nonetheless out of his control.

> At that subtle moment when man glances backward over his life, Sisyphus returning toward his rock, in that slight pivoting he contemplates that series of unrelated actions which becomes his fate, created by him, combined under his memory's eye and soon sealed by his death. Thus, convinced of the wholly human origin of all that is human, a blind man eager to see who knows that the night holds no end, he is still on the go, the rock is still rolling.[18]

The clear break in the illusion of control and the desire to establish causality forces Sisyphus to attain a new understanding of human limitations. Once emancipated from the illusion that he is master over his own life and that events follow a clear chain of causality, Sisyphus becomes liberated even in the midst of punishment everlasting. Job also gave up on his ability to understand and was comforted. However, ultimately the book of Job reneges upon this message by rewarding Job handsomely, reestablishing the causal link between obedience to God and divine law and reward. Camus goes one step further and suggests it is the hoax of causality and perception that is our true punishment. The suffering caused by this single proclivity may indeed outweigh all other kinds of misfortune.

So why exactly is man's life a prison? Because of the seemingly inescapable drive to create order that *will* disintegrate, just as Sisyphus's boulder rolls down the hill again? Because we see punishment everywhere around us where there is only random suffering? Because we create orders to punish us in ways that are comprehensible, perhaps with the intention of occluding the pain and suffering that ultimately defy perceptible order? All three of these dynamics pervade our experiences and help explain the prisons and rules we carry within and create for ourselves and one another. Punishment emerges as the key to understanding why and how we create and re-create political order.

CHAPTER 3

Earthly Divinity

Punishment and the Requirements of Sovereignty

> That kind of man-made irreality—indeed, that strange construction of a
> human mind which finally becomes slave to its own fictions—we are nor-
> mally more ready to find in the religious sphere than in the allegedly sober
> and realistic realms of law, politics, and constitution . . .
> —Ernst H. Kantorowicz, *The King's Two Bodies*

I began this book by rejecting the simple equation of the power to punish and the power of command, and in drawing a connection between
punishment and sovereignty I risk the appearance of endorsing this
very position. What I offer is a more complicated, and more complete,
view of the relationship between sovereignty and punishment. Due to
the influence of theorists such as Michel Foucault and Giorgio Agamben, as well as recent historical events, sovereignty has come to be
understood as an unstoppable force often trampling the law in its violent assertions. However, examining the history of the concept of sovereignty and its evolution, one finds surprising fragility. Sovereignty is
based upon representation and perception, and is therefore vulnerable
in regard to its audience. To be sure, it hides this vulnerability well
since sovereignty could not successfully provide and enforce political
order if the source of its power were easily discernible. Punishment
may display the power behind politics today, but a different perspective reveals much of the scurrying that is happening behind stage to
orchestrate this spectacle. While the common understanding is that
sovereignty and punishment are mutually constitutive, I argue that
strategies of representation are the forgotten element in this equation.
Adding this third term into consideration fundamentally shifts our
understanding of the relationship between punishment and sovereignty. Though sovereignty may be the central tool of modern political

orders, it is nonetheless susceptible to the perceptions of those whose lives it seeks to order.

There has been a flurry of newly released theoretical works that address the problem of sovereignty.[1] A common conjecture is that in our political era, there has been a significant shift in the form and practice of sovereignty. Some have argued that the practice of nation-state sovereignty has become eroded through international administration and institutions, global capitalism, and militarism. Others hold that sovereignty has become even stronger, in the sense that the individual rights that formerly held it in check are now waning in their power of resistance. Against the tenor of much of this scholarship, this chapter explores the more consistent aspects of sovereignty. For even as history unfolds in a dynamic fashion, there are defining aspects of political order that remain present. As sovereignty is one of the key elements of political order (if not the most), understanding how it is constituted, expressed, and maintained is an integral element of this book's endeavor. This is not to say that the expression and practice of sovereignty have been unaltered, only that basic elements nonetheless remain constant.

The fascinating aspect of sovereignty is how firm a grasp on social order is exerted by something so intangible. Modern political orders adopted the notion of sovereignty, inspired by the divine power that had, if incompletely, provided some order in the world. Otherworldly powers are not as evidently fallible as worldly ones, and less contestable. Political sovereignty is a worldly power, but how can an admittedly man-made construction garner the same power as a divine entity? To order the world, a sovereign power must be of it yet simultaneously transcend it. It is tempting to overlook the ethereal aspects of sovereignty lurking behind the sometimes monstrous exertions in its name. But in many ways, the power garnered by modern sovereignty stems from its transcendent nature.

Sovereignty can be described as a self-contained dialectic: it is understood as transcendent yet needs to be actualized. It achieves the reconciliation of these opposing forces through representation that must establish it as a force or presence distinct from all others. While political sovereignty was directly linked with God, there was no question of authority. By locating political authority on earth and making it corporeal, modern sovereignty becomes potentially fallible. The modern sovereign must have a human face but must also be more than human to serve as the boundary of political order, the guarantor of the lives of others. It must be simultaneously human but perfect; worldly yet superhuman in order to protect subjects from one another.

We have seen how human reason demanded the development of the Leviathan, a creature to redeem suffering and provide comprehensible order. The shape of this figure perfectly fulfills the needs of sovereignty as superhuman, yet earthly. Because Hobbes explicitly unmasks his demigod as an "Artificiall Man" we often think that the form, but not the substance, of mysticism persists in early modern politics. Yet the demands of sovereignty require that traces of divine privilege remain to order the polity.

Through punishment, sovereignty comes to be represented. The question is, how does a sovereign exercise power but still maintain the trace of divinity or that which is more than mortal? Doesn't the manifestation of power in the practice of punishment pose a risk to the otherworldly status of the sovereign? Agamben and Foucault have focused on the ordering capacities of sovereignty, emphasizing its extreme strength in the face of those subject to it. Because punishment is where sovereignty becomes most evident, it is also where it risks the source of its own power. In embodying and manifesting this "divine power" so concretely, punishment can make the demi-God, in Nietzsche's words, become human, all too human.

To understand how punishment both constitutes and threatens modern sovereignty, I begin with an examination of the origins and development of the term *sovereignty* and revive the representational and perceptual elements. Taking the issue of representation as key, I look at sovereignty's relationship to law and institutions of governmentality in practices of punishment as proposed by Schmitt, Agamben, and Foucault. Using their discussions as a point of departure, we can look at practices of punishment not only as a material expression of the power of sovereignty but also as a strategy of maintaining distance between the sovereign and the punishment done in its name. The sovereign must punish to assert power, but these same practices of punishment must reveal the transcendental aspects of sovereignty. This is a difficult balance to achieve, and it makes punishment the most crucial undertaking of a sovereign power. A concluding discussion of Camus' "Reflections on the Guillotine" demonstrates how the expressions of the force of sovereignty also reveal the vulnerabilities of modern political order.

Sovereignty

In the *Oxford English Dictionary*, one finds that the word *sovereign* was used during the late fourteenth century to mean divine authority over the earth and its inhabitants, the power of a man over his wife or of fathers over their children, as well as the power of a king over his subjects. Interestingly, it was also used to designate someone who was superior to others within the same class, someone who is truly exceptional, simultaneously belonging to yet standing apart from a particular category. The simultaneity of these different uses suggests it is erroneous to designate the divine form of sovereignty as medieval and the worldly one as modern, since sovereignty was understood as having both transcendental and worldly origins.

Nonetheless, we can see that the worldly origins of sovereignty came to be more important with the establishment of secular regimes, and that this form of sovereignty continues to have a central role to play in the establishment, legitimation, and perpetuation of political regimes. Hardt and Negri's work *Empire* includes a short passage on the nature of modern sovereignty. While they detail the concept in order to prove that it is eroding, their observations are still an excellent place to begin.

> Sovereignty is thus defined both by *transcendence* and by *representation*, two concepts that the humanist tradition has posed as contradictory. On the one hand, the transcendence of the sovereign is founded not on an external theological support but only on the immanent logic of human relations. On the other hand, the representation that functions to legitimate this sovereign power also alienates it completely from the multitude of subjects.[2]

This description beautifully evokes the paradoxical nature of sovereignty, though I do not think that it necessarily is limited to modern sovereignty as they suggest. Sovereignty is something that exists above and beyond what is immediately apparent. We may not see divine majesty, but we see different occurrences as proof of his grace or displeasure. In other words, we look to the world to confirm that which exists outside of it. It is a curious fact that we are willing to adopt such a stance even toward ideals that do not threaten us with the ultimate punishment or reward of hell or heaven.

Recognizing the awkward corporality of a king who is supposed to stand for something much greater than a mere mortal, English jurisprudence of the Tudor period developed an understanding that the king had two bodies, one which was mortal, the other immortal and political. This was an ingenious solution to the problem of the need for permanent sovereignty accompanied by a worldly embodiment, the perfect illustration of what Hardt and Negri note is the simultaneously immanent and transcendent presence of sovereignty. Kantorowicz describes the innovative law in *The King's Two Bodies*.

> For the King has in him two Bodies, viz., a Body natural, and a Body politic. His Body natural (if it be considered in itself) is a Body mortal, subject to all Infirmities that come by Nature or Accident, to the Imbecility of Infancy or of old Age, and the like Defects that happen to the natural Bodies of other People. But his Body politic is a Body that cannot be seen or handled, consisting of Policy and Government, and constituted for the Direction of the People, and the Management of the public weal, and this Body is utterly void of Infancy, and old Age, and other natural Defects and Imbecilities, which the Body natural is subject to, and for this Cause, what the King does in his Body politic, cannot be invalidated or frustrated by any Disability in his natural Body.[3]

Rarely has there been such an excellent demonstration of the necessity of rescuing transcendental order from the vulgarities of raw materiality. Kantorowicz observes that the utility of the device is that the imagined political body of the king always supersedes the failures or incapacities of the natural body. Transcendent fiction mitigates flawed fact.

Representation is the primary means by which the transcendent becomes manifest. Here the presupposed empiricism of law helps to establish the fiction of the king's two bodies as fact. Every system of sovereignty utilizes a system of representation and perception. Paradoxically, signifying the transcendent in recognizable ways relies upon systems of perception, visuality, and knowledge that are immanent. This is the aspect of their own definition that Hardt and Negri fail to explore. For they say that the representation itself tends to create distance between the sovereign and those beneath it. Yet the sovereign is created through perception. Representing sovereignty is not enough to establish it; instead the *perception* of sovereignty as it is represented is the key.

The truly miraculous nature of sovereignty is its self-referentiality, and the power it gains through this process. The sovereign defines itself as the supreme power and then creates a system of political order to sustain itself as such. Foucault observed, "In every case, what characterizes the end of sovereignty, this common and general good, is in sum nothing other than submission to sovereignty. This means that the exercise of sovereignty is circular: the end of sovereignty is the exercise of sovereignty. The good is obedience to the law, hence the good for sovereignty is that people should obey it."[4] In short, one becomes sovereign because one claims it and can represent oneself as such in a relatively convincing fashion. The end of sovereignty is the preservation of sovereignty at all costs: sovereignty is both the means and end of political order.

Despite the multiple usages of the term, sovereignty still enjoys a unique position when thinking about power. In all of these cases, it is power that declares itself such and is accepted as supreme. In fact, one may be sovereign without having done anything except appear as sovereign. Sovereignty is a status and a norm rather than an action. For instance, a military commander holds the powers of life and death over her soldiers, yet this does not make her their sovereign, even though they are trained to obey without question. Conversely, a lame-duck executive may not be able to rule as he did before an election but is sovereign in the given territory until the term officially expires. These two examples suggest that it is not merely the ability or inability to command that makes one sovereign. Instead it is the belief in these exclusive powers by those subject to and embodying sovereignty that creates it.

In *The Province of Jurisprudence Determined*, John Austin observes that sovereignty must have three qualities—be accepted, perceptible, and beyond restriction: "The habitual obedience to the government which is rendered by the bulk of the community, partly arises, therefore in almost every society, from the cause which I now have described: namely, a perception of the bulk of the community of the utility of political government, or a preference by the bulk of the community of any government to anarchy."[5] For practical reasons, people desire government. But this government only acquires the form of sovereignty when it defines itself as such. Austin points out that sovereignty is human, must be determinate, and must be recognized as sovereign, and that the society itself must be defined as political and independent. "If a determinate human superior, not in a habit of obedience to a like superior, receive habitual obedience from the bulk of a given society, that determinate superior is sovereign in that society, and the society (including the superior) is a society political and independent."[6]

What defines a political order is the existence of the sovereign. What makes one sovereign is to not be subject to any other human superior, as well as be recognizable as the sovereign. This much seems clear: the power of the sovereign establishes political and legal order. But there is one more element here—the habitual obedience of the sovereign. Austin argued that the society must have already established the practice of obeying; otherwise the advantages of, for example, the social contract, would not be evident. As Charles Merriam observed, "Custom is not law, it is true, until it is endorsed by the sovereign; but on the other hand, the sovereign is not sovereign until recognized by custom. Habitual obedience, the custom of obeying, constitutes the fundamental and essential basis of the political society and of the supreme power."[7] What would generate the custom of obedience other than punishment? Punishment emerges as the grounds of the unity of law and power in the concept of sovereignty.

Punishment generates the custom of accepting authority and demonstrating its advantages even in the absence of express consent. Furthermore, the practice of punishment provides the habits of obedience not just in those being punished but in all those who accept the authority's right to punish. It is the custom of obedience that creates the perception of authority, serving as the grounds for the more formal codification of a social order into a political one. From the habits of the whip come the legitimation of the law and the subsequent transformation of the earthly sovereign into something much grander than its origins.

It may seem all too simple to generate the habits of obedience and thus cultivate sovereignty through punishment. But it is important to remember that the representation of sovereignty must contain elements of the transcendental. How can punishment be used to represent the sovereign without coming to embody it and thereby compromise its unique status? The particular challenges of establishing and exercising sovereignty were noted by Foucault: "This means that, whereas the doctrine of the prince and the juridical theory of sovereignty are constantly attempting to draw the line between the power of the prince and any other form of power, because its task is to explain and justify this essential discontinuity between them, in the art of government the task is to establish a continuity, in both an upwards and a downwards direction."[8] The power of the prince and the state in general must appear to be distinct from all other forms of power, as well as those people who act in its name. In this way, the understanding of sovereignty as transcendental helps to accomplish the necessary segregation of state power from all other forms of social control. The need to use other forms of power, yet remain distinct from these implements, demonstrates why representation becomes the central element in the balance of sovereignty. Representation must distinguish sovereignty from its embodiment, whether it is a contract, population, person, or law. For this reason, the representation of sovereignty as transcendental is just as important as the representation of the sovereign as all-powerful.

Punishment may generate obedience, but it relies upon laws, executioners, prisons, and other instruments to do so. In examining practices of punishment we see the difficult balance between the maintenance of sovereignty's ethereal status, combined with the need to have a worldly embodiment of sovereign might. The law and institutions of punishment have been two primary methods by which sovereignty has maintained paradoxical presence. In these next two sections, I will be drawing on the work of Foucault, Agamben, and Schmitt, who also looked at the constitution and exercise of sovereignty in relationship to law and institutions.

Sovereign Exceptionalism in Law and Punishment

The concern with creating a political power that was strong enough to enforce social and political order is what drove the earliest modern conceptions of sovereignty. Jean Bodin, confronted with the rebellion of the Huguenots in sixteenth-century France, insisted that sovereignty had to be both indivisible and absolute. However, the need to have a worldly embodiment of sovereignty caused a problem in modern philosophy from the beginning. Bodin, writing about the absolute, indivisible power of the sovereign, was confronted by the empirical proof that the sovereign was indeed limited. As one commentator noted, "the gap between the abstract fiction of his lawful sovereign and what he conceived to be the reality of the actual constitutional position of the King of France remains astonishingly and revealingly wide."[9] As the consolidation of France under a central authority remained tenuous, in his 1576 work on sovereignty Bodin insisted that consent was immaterial.

"We thus see that the main point of sovereign majesty and absolute power consists of giving the law to subjects in general without their consent."[10] The authority of the sovereign was inherent in the concept itself and by definition contingent upon neither consent nor law. Bodin, considered the father of modern sovereignty, developed his understanding of the term according to what was required by his era. He is not an apologist for absolutism but rather argues in favor of absolutism, which did not at the time effectively exist.

Even more revealing, Bodin argued that the appearance of sovereignty was misleading. In its essence it was infallible, no matter how flawed or limited it appeared. In example after example, Bodin admits that in particular times and circumstances, it may appear that power is divided or that the king exists in a subservient position to the law. Nonetheless, he insists *by his own definition of sovereignty* that these scenarios are simply impossible. Bodin is a prime example of a philosopher willing the world to exist in a fashion that it clearly did not. Hence, looking at the theory of sovereignty in historical context, there is a great distinction between the empirical workings of sovereignty and the normative understanding of it. Serving as the intermediary step between the fragility of political regimes and the fiction of absolute power was the juridical-legal system.

The law helped to provide the empirical confirmation of the fiction of the king's two bodies in medieval English law. Here, Bodin moves one further step, using the law itself as the device with which to bridge the gap between fact and norm. This analysis reverses the one posited by Michel Foucault in his lectures at the Collège de France published under the title *"Society Must Be Defended."* Here, Foucault argues that there was a switch from late medieval forms of sovereignty that were aligned with the king's body and largely exercised upon the bodies of his subjects. In an argument reflected in *Discipline and Punish,* Foucault points out that the juridical forms of sovereignty that come after this period are more focused on land and maximizing productive capabilities. He implies that the juridical apparatus is only a cover for the ever-increasing administration of bodies, however. "One might say that once disciplinary constraints had to both function as mechanisms of domination and be concealed to the extent that they were the mode in which power was actually exercised, the theory of sovereignty had to find expression in the juridical apparatus and had to be reactivated or complemented by judicial codes."[11] Here he implies that judicial codes made a new kind of sovereignty possible, one that utilized disciplinary mechanisms while at the same time invoking rights. Legality is viewed as an ideological cover for a dominating and extracting political power.

On the contrary, one finds when examining Bodin that legality serves as the empirical referent for the fiction of absolute power. In reality, worldly sovereignty is limited and fallible; it needs the political fictions of theorists as well as the law to establish the power of the sovereign as infallible. The exclusive alliance made between sovereignty and law sets sovereignty apart from other forms of domination, but not just because it can then cloak itself in the guise of legality. The law defines sovereignty as such and, since Bodin, has provided its primary empirical referent: it makes the transcendental aspects of modern sovereignty worldly in its power.

Restated in other terms, sovereignty is a problem of how to relate what Foucault calls two different ways of analyzing power, "the juridical schema" whereby power is constituted and circumscribed by the law, or the "domination-repression schema" whereby power is achieved or resisted in terms of struggle and submission.[12] While Foucault argues that the oppressive-dominating effects of power lurk beneath the juridical apparatus, Schmitt argues that the two aspects are intertwined in the concept of sovereignty. After all, *sovereignty* is a juridical term that is nonetheless meaningless without the ability to act and to wield authority. That such actions are not then subject to the same judicial oversight, no matter how egregiously they offend written law, is what Schmitt refers to as the sovereign exception. Schmitt's analysis states that sovereign power, not law, is ultimately what matters.

Schmitt believes all political concepts are adopted from religious, theological ones. Modern sovereignty is no exception.

> All significant concepts of the modern theory of the state are secularized theological concepts not only because of their historical development—in which they were transferred from theology to the theory of the state, whereby, for example, the omnipotent God became the omnipotent lawgiver—but also because of their systemic structure, the recognition of which is necessary for a sociological consideration of these concepts. The exception in jurisprudence is analogous to the miracle in theology.[13]

Schmitt argues that the transport of sovereignty from heaven to earth is not only driven by historical development but also reflects a switch in metaphysics. Immanence, not transcendence, becomes the defining aspect of modern sovereignty. This basic view guides Schmitt's view of the relationship between sovereignty and law, with sovereignty standing for worldly power and law as an idealistic construction.

Bodin's work suggests that the empiricism of the law is used to transform the fiction of sovereignty into a historical force. Schmitt's argument offers a twist on this logic by stating that law is fiction, while sovereignty is real. The fact that the sovereign can suspend the law proves that law is contingent upon sovereignty, not the reverse. Even though typically the rule of law provides the basis for everyday governance, the exception proves that the sovereign is ultimately superior. Take, for example, a state of emergency when typical legal or legislative procedures are suspended. Only the sovereign may determine whether such a state of emergency has arisen. Even more tellingly, when the law is suspended, the sovereign still rules.

The transformation into a political order based upon immanence is also accomplished by the establishment of juridical principles that will lead to a routinization of political order. The goal of modern constitutionalism is to encompass all contingencies and thereby prevent any occurrences that could potentially fall outside of the law. For this reason, the law itself specifies under what conditions and exactly how it can be suspended. In this way, even the lapse of the law appears as its own confirmation. However, as Schmitt points out, the state of emergency that requires the suspension of law reveals the true workings of sovereignty. "What characterizes an exception is principally unlimited authority, which means the suspension of the entire working order."[14] The law itself, in conformity and assuming a norm, cannot determine whether such a norm exists. Instead, sovereignty, the power that stands outside yet is reinforced by the law, "definitively decides whether this normal situation actually exists."[15] Because order persists, even when the law is suspended, *in practice* sovereignty clearly provides the basis for political order. Sovereignty, no matter how well it is defined, rationalized, divided, or confirmed, does not have any substantial meaning outside of its exercise. Schmitt argues that the *exercise* rather than the definition of sovereignty reveals its mechanics.

Undoubtedly, Schmitt is correct in offering this assessment of the mechanics of sovereignty. There are times when the sovereign suspends the law, and the ability to punish itself can be seen as exhibiting an exceptional relationship to the law. The fact that the state can incarcerate while all others cannot demonstrates the paradoxical relationship Schmitt describes: the sovereign is not subject to the laws in the same way as all other entities and can therefore guarantee the rule of law.

The work of Giorgio Agamben takes Schmitt's insights and applies them to recent political events and also trends in the twentieth century. Agamben observes that these "exceptional" demonstrations of power gradually become the rule. He also points out that one expression of the power of the sovereign is that it can decide which populations are governed by the rule of law and which are not. Schmitt's exceptionalism can also be applied to populations, in addition to standard legal proceduralism. Agamben's argument seems particularly relevant today given the diffusion of special extralegal categories such as enemy combatant, and the definition of physical spaces in which political power can be exercised without any tempering by international human rights or domestic legal regulations. Thinking of sovereignty as a force that is only imperfectly tempered by the rule of law, Agamben's view of sovereignty as an unstoppable power creeping over the entire globe feels scary and prescient.

Agamben does point to real dynamics in contemporary politics. However, he also overstates the power of sovereignty. After all, at times the exercise of even sovereign exceptionalism has brought censorship and removal from office, international outrage, or popular rebellion. If sovereignty were able to define its own terms as completely as Schmitt and Agamben would have us believe, the Soviet Union would still be intact and all "democratic" elections would be purely theatrical or usually suspended if they posed the risk of producing a regime change.

The fact is that sovereignty can be taken away, and it can be risked through its exercise. If the ability to exercise power were enough to generate sovereignty, political history would be a tediously constant narrative. There are instability and uncertainty, however. Part of this is due to the requirements of sovereignty to both order a polity yet remain aloof from it as well. Bodin's originating work offers us a new way of thinking about the rule of law and sovereignty today. The ability to suspend the law, to exercise clemency, or to determine which populations are more vulnerable may also be a way of signaling the transcendental elements of the sovereign. It alone can stand apart from legal order, and it becomes a power entirely unique through this privilege. The effects of this unique relationship are all too real, and often tragic or deadly.

Yet sovereignty is still vulnerable. Punishment poses a very particular challenge for the exercise of sovereign power: to demonstrate and uphold the rule of law, the sovereign must provide sanctions. Yet punishment cannot become personal or viewed as merely a way of maintaining power, otherwise it seems a product of worldly calculations and limitations, not a semidivine presence. It must be allied with the transcendental order if sovereignty is not to become weakened. The concluding chapter of this book will examine this hypothesis in more detail with an examination of current U.S. penal practices at home and abroad. The central issue, made crystal clear in the practice of state punishment, is how sovereignty can order yet transcend the world. In many ways, you can look at the development of bureaucratic elements of political rule as a strategy to minimize the risk in exercising sovereignty, as I explain in the next section.

The Disciplinary Articulation of Sovereignty

The ability to suspend the law through exceptionalism, providing clemency, or even defining which populations can be sacrificed is one way that sovereign power establishes itself as transcendent vis-à-vis the law. Another method for establishing this simultaneously transcendent and immanent presence is by separating the executive powers of sovereignty from their administration. This is the dynamic of sovereignty that captures the attention of Michel Foucault. Foucault's work investigates the teleological development of the power of sovereignty toward a disciplinary regime and, finally, what he terms *governmentality*. He offers a trio of terms—sovereignty, government, discipline—and explores the evolving nature of their interrelationship. Initially, sovereignty, which he understands largely as a judicial construct, utilizes a system of punishment and violence to embody the power of the king. As sovereignty is embodied in the king, when a crime occurs, the king himself is considered the injured party. Like the laws themselves, the punishment must reflect both the immanent and transcendent bodies of the king. Here is Foucault's description: "Now, this portion belonging to the prince is not in itself simple; on the one hand, it requires redress for the injury that has been done his kingdom (as an element of disorder and as an example given to others, this considerable injury is out of all proportion to that which has been committed upon a private individual); but it also requires that the king take revenge for an affront to his very person."[16] In the practice of punishment, particularly in the era of spectacular corporal punishment, the full complexity of the king's sovereignty is acted out and reconstituted upon the body of the condemned.

However, Foucault points out that this practice was ultimately unstable. The bloody spectacular display of sovereign power actually created more violence and destabilized, rather than consolidated, the power of the sovereign. Perhaps the too literal embodiment of the transcendental in such gruesome fashion made it more difficult to sustain the fiction of sovereignty. Interestingly, this was one of Locke's primary objections to absolutist forms of government. When the king is always party to the crime, as he is when he and sovereignty are singular, the punishment will always carry a tinge of revenge. As both party to the crime and judge and executioner, rationality cannot be maintained, hence punishment only extends the state of war rather than reestablishing the power of the social compact. Locke's observation is borne out by Foucault's studies of the disorder of the mob at public punishments.

Foucault's oeuvre suggests that sovereignty was redefined along with the methods of punishment that represented it. With the development of popular sovereignty came the acute necessity for the development of discipline. *Discipline and Punish* explores the historical development of a new penal apparatus along with shifts in government methods to enforce this discipline. Because he describes to such great effect how sovereignty becomes dispersed and ultimately a matter of self-discipline, the overall outlook of this particular work of Foucault's is rather bleak. Once again, it seems as though there is nowhere one can escape the sovereign power, and resistance is futile. But Rousseau's *Social Contract* can be read as a companion volume to this work, as it describes the internalization and social control in the terms of the freedom gained through popular sovereignty.

It is crucial to remember why the administration of the population that Foucault describes to such horrific effect was considered a movement toward freedom. It is not that the false promise of personal freedom was able to blind many generations to the increasing power of sovereignty. Rather, self-governance was understood as a form of self-control (the connections between democratic practice and punishment shall be explored in full detail in the next chapter). What is important to note here is that the changes Foucault describes reflect a vision of popular sovereignty, a fact that becomes occluded in his own discussion. Sovereignty is the one aspect of Foucault's triangular configuration that remains static, and he implies that it loses its importance except as an ideological cover for the increase of disciplinary practices.

Foucault looks at a fundamental reorientation away from what he describes as a sovereignty-based state, to a disciplinary society—one in which power is more productive and conducive to political economy. This shift ends in governmentality, an era of complete administration upheld by institutions in and outside of the state. Foucault describes governmentality as "the process, or rather, the result of the process, through which the state of justice of the Middle Ages, transformed into the administrative state during the fifteenth and sixteenth centuries, gradually becomes governmentalized."[17] Sovereignty then comes to legitimate itself based upon the sanctity of the body and the protection of the rights of citizens, rather than the sanctity of the ruler. This requires a new form of social control that seeks to maximize the productive capacities of its citizens. The development of various institutions of education, penality, and health helps to create and administer the population of the modern state. The sovereign power of the state has become increasingly effective at utilizing institutions that appear to be independent.

In this way, the transcendence of the sovereign state is maintained, while the exercise of its power has only increased. Because the sovereign is so removed from the actions done in its name, its exercise generates virtually no resistance. Foucault's basic insight is that an invisible and decentralized power is able to exercise greater control than an embodied one. The primary concern is how changes in the form of government have created regimes that have almost complete control over the human body, a process that he terms *biopolitics*.

Foucault's work adds two new elements to this discussion of punishment and the requirements of sovereignty. First, the development of a disciplinary apparatus certainly reduces the potential of generating resistance through the exercise of sovereign powers. But the separation between the act of punishing and the ability to wield sovereignty needs to be noted. The common understanding is that the exercise of sovereignty through punishment is its constitution, as in Agamben's and Schmitt's works. Foucault's work suggests a rather startling evolution, that the act of punishing does not generate sovereignty at all. If it did, the prison guard would be sovereign. Instead, she does not perceive herself as such, nor do others, even though she is exercising the classic power of command. While modern sovereignty may use a greater variety of tools to manifest itself, Foucault's discussion reveals that sovereignty is still reliant upon perception rather than any particular action or capacity. Sovereignty cannot be traced only by the actions done in its name. We also need to pay close attention to its strategies of self-representation, which is particularly revealing in cases of punishment. Here the orchestration of the perception of the sovereign becomes visible, and crucial if the power is not to become overly worldly and limited.

Second, while Foucault's discussion of sovereignty and power suggests that both become stronger through dispersion, a constant relationship to the law remains intact. The disciplinarity that Foucault describes suggests that all of us somehow become instruments of sovereignty. But sovereignty itself is still distinguished by a particular relationship to the law. Consider the difference between vigilantism and the exercise of disciplinarity described by Foucault. If the point would be to have the most pervasive implementation of the interests of the sovereign, vigilantism would certainly help in accomplishing the task. Mobs could enforce discipline and thereby increase the sovereign rule. At times social reprisals would be a more effective deterrent against future crime than state-sanctioned procedures. If it was only about adherence to the law, vigilantism could be embraced as a partner in, if not substitute for, state punishment. Instead, it is officially prohibited. Admittedly, at times vigilantism is tolerated and even encouraged by state officials,[18] but the practice cannot be officially sanctioned because to do so would relinquish the sovereign's unique relationship to the law. It is the strategic representation and perception of this relationship to the law that remains the source of sovereign power.

These two observations are linked. Sovereignty is able to represent itself and be perceived as distinct from other expressions of force through a unique relationship to the law. This requirement remains even at the moment when it appears that sovereign power becomes most manifest, in the act of disciplining bodies. The requirements of sovereignty in the act of punishing are then taxing—it becomes particularly vulnerable given the need to demonstrate an allegiance to the law during the exercise of force.

Camus: Sovereignty Unveiled

This body of literature on sovereignty that emphasizes the power of sovereign exceptionalism, the diffusion of its instruments, and the consolidation of its power demonstrates how successful this hybrid concept has been in constructing the basis of modern political power. Yet there is instability in the relationship between punishment and sovereignty that needs to be exposed. Albert Camus' "Reflections on the Guillotine," a complex and masterful rhetorical piece against capital punishment, also reveals something essential about the exercise and nature of modern state sovereignty. Capital punishment displays the exclusive prerogatives of the state but simultaneously risks its unique authority through its exercise. After all, if state punishment were simply a matter of exercising power, it would not have spawned the intricate legal codes and machinery for assistance. Camus' discussion more than any other I have encountered reveals the methods by which sovereignty can be undone through its punishment practices.

Camus begins his essay with a story.

> Shortly before the war of 1914, an assassin whose crime was particularly repulsive (he had slaughtered a family of farmers, including the children) was condemned to death in Algiers. He was a farm worker who had killed in a sort of bloodthirsty frenzy but had aggravated his case by robbing his victims. The affair created a great stir. It was generally thought that decapitation was too mild a punishment for such a monster. This was the opinion, I have been told, of my father, who was especially aroused by the murder of the children. One of the few things I know about him, in any case, is that he wanted to witness the execution at the other end of town amid a great crowd of people. What he saw that morning he never told anyone. My mother relates merely that he came rushing home, his face distorted, refused to talk, lay down for a moment on the bed, and suddenly began to vomit. He had just discovered the reality hidden under the noble phrases with which it was masked. Instead of thinking of the slaughtered children, he could think of nothing but that quivering body that had just been dropped onto a board to have its head cut off.[19]

Camus starts with the story to replace the abstract pronouncements of justice with descriptions of severed heads that still have the power of vision and limbs that jump during burial. He points out that even though punishment is justified through tradition, the impartial application of the law, and procedural administration, we still use language to occlude the reality of administering pain. We say "justice has been served" when someone has been sentenced to life in prison or death, and "the prisoner" and "the condemned" become figures with no identity outside of his or her status. Camus wants to emphasize the materiality of punishment, pointing out that these are bodies in pain. The gruesome reality will belie the noble phrases if we are forced to contend with the fact that "the condemned" is not a position in a justice system but rather a living being. Camus' strategy is to illuminate the practice of capital punishment, contending it cannot stand close examination.

If punishment were only about the demonstration of sovereign power, Camus' strategy would have little effect and in fact would backfire. If the ability to punish constructs the power of the sovereign, then describing it in detail would only make that power seem more formidable. Instead, Camus' hunch is correct: the more closely we examine practices of punishment, the more fallible modern sovereignty appears. Camus' strategy works because the nature of sovereignty demands certain opacity.

The processes of state punishment are done in the name of the law or state, but those who administer them do not occupy positions of power. I have argued why this is a necessary aspect of sovereignty and that punishment must make it operable without becoming limited. Punishment occurs in the name of the sovereign without becoming overly manifest in the figure of guard, judge, or even executioner. In "Civil Disobedience," Henry David Thoreau described the division particularly clearly. He observed that the jailers serve the state "as machines, with their bodies" while those who make the laws and policy serve the state with "their heads"—it is the division of the two, body and mind, that eases culpability for those who do punish and those that command it.[20] Asserting the individual identity of the person who administers punishment disturbs this configuration by insisting upon his or her human identity. Camus understands this dynamic and exploits it in his essay against capital punishment, by relaying the diaries and feelings of those who administer sovereign power.

Camus describes two different responses in those who administer the penal system. On the one hand, we have those who cannot bear their involvement in such activities. "Just listen then to the warden of an English prison who confesses to 'a keen sense of personal shame' and to the chaplain who speaks of 'horror, shame, and humiliation'" (195). The cruelty of capital punishment in particular, and all punishment in general, affects not only the faceless guilty ones, but also the deliberately nameless people who administer it. Even more disturbing are Camus' descriptions of those who like to deliver the punishment. An executioner's assistant writes in his journal, "The new executioner is batty about the guillotine. He sometimes spends days on end at home sitting on a chair, ready with hat and coat on, waiting for a summons from the Ministry." There are also overly eager citizens, ready to participate in the due punishment of the condemned: Camus reports that "hundreds of persons offer to serve as executioners without pay" (196). The fact that those who punish exhibit emotion, regret, *or* anticipation destroys the illusion of punishment as a mechanical process. But sovereignty must deploy mankind as its tools: we are complicit, not separate.

Camus points out that capital punishment has become ever more hidden from view to hide the fact of human agency. The same is true of all punishment today in the United States. If a prison guard were to acquire a face, we could look and find indifference in the face of suffering, an anguished soul, or sadism: any of these options would disturb our sense of the administration of punishment tempered by law and institutional mechanisms, therefore we choose again and again to obscure any specifics. We like the idea of the machinery of justice but recoil when presented with a concrete example, as in Kafka's "In the Penal Colony."

While much of Camus' essay is a case against capital punishment, for the purpose of this argument the most revealing passages come when he links the practice of capital punishment with state sovereignty. He has detailed how capital punishment fails to deter, he has demonstrated that capital punishment potentially destabilizes the representation of the state as a benevolent or at least neutral party, and therefore it hides the practice away from the public eye. This is not a spectacular representation of state sovereignty; instead, sovereignty represents itself as hidden, invisible—as is appropriate to maintain the aura of transcendence through impartial administration.

Since the practice of punishment places such a stress on this system, one would assume that the practice of punishment would be lessened or avoided. On the contrary, the state must take on the mantle of punishment. Camus points out how the practices of punishment become integrally linked to the self-conception of the state and the nature of the power it demands for itself. At one time, the state punished—with death and other penalties—in the name of religious values or deities. When the state serves the interests of the divine, its punishments can be seen as a sort of intermediary step, not the ultimate end in itself. Camus points out that for true believers, even today, capital punishment is "a temporary penalty that leaves the final sentence in suspense, an arrangement necessary only for terrestrial order, an administrative measure which, far from signifying the end for the guilty man, may instead favor his redemption" (224).

The last chapter displayed how modern sovereignty moved from punishment in the name of unearthly order to the earthly divinity described in this chapter. The state still punishes, and must do so to provide this "terrestrial order," but it does so in its own name, in the name of a worldly order. As Camus points out, this makes those who administer punishments hypocritical: they do it in the name of a God they don't believe in. But in fact, the very act of punishing asserts human political order over a divine one. No matter whether the blade is drawn in the name of God or the law of state, it establishes the sovereign on earth. And this sovereign becomes visible through its manifestations.

Camus' piercing critique of capital punishment amounts to this: that the state punishes in the name of absolute right, and that the power to punish is essentially godlike, but the force is exerted without faith. Instead, punishment happens in the name of reason, knowledge, and information—not mystical faith. "Europe's malady consists in believing nothing and claiming to know everything" (229). With the secularization of state order, the state had to punish in its own name. But the ability and right to punish cannot be grounded in something as worldly as knowledge and reason. They are too fallible. For instance, clear rationales can be provided for differing views, knowledge does change, and information is less than perfect. How can we then use these secular tools as the basis of administering pain? On the other hand, there is no choice if political power is to have secular grounds.

Camus has unveiled the unstable foundations of modern sovereignty: it is secular, but assumes the powers of a god. For this reason, whenever sovereignty is revealed as human, fallible, it becomes threatened. This is why it is particularly important to deny the impulse to see sovereignty as the overwhelming mechanism described by Foucault, Agamben, and Schmitt. This perception of sovereignty as otherworldly only strengthens it. As Camus observes and demonstrates in this essay, once punishment is viewed in all of its materiality, both the condemned and the administrator become all too human, interfering with the current justifications for sovereign power. Inherent in the form of modern sovereignty is a check on its exercise: if it becomes too earthly or exposed as human, it ceases to have the same power. Therefore we must look at punishment as an expression of sovereign power, and not be awed by its strength, though it certainly does exhibit tremendous force at times. We must be willing to look closely in order to expose its weakness. After all, it is nothing without the hand that holds the key, the judge that shuffles the papers, and the person who chooses whether or not to file charges. Our perception is what creates the power of sovereignty; that same perception can and should contest its absolutist claims.

CHAPTER 4

Severing the Sanguinary Empire

Punishment and Early American Democratic Idealism

> Lay then the axe to the root, and teach governments humanity. It is their
> sanguinary punishments which corrupt mankind.
> —Thomas Paine, *The Rights of Man*

The opinion rendered by Justice Kennedy in *Roper v. Simmons* on March
1, 2005, that finds capital punishment for crimes committed while the
offender was a juvenile to be cruel and unusual contains an unusually
exact historical reversal. The ruling was bolstered by recent psychological research that establishes moral capacities are not fully developed in
late adolescence. The decision was largely anticipated on the strength
of this particular argument following the 2004 decision to stop execution of the mentally impaired. However, there is another line of argu-
mentation advanced by Justice Kennedy. He notes that many states
within the United States have banned capital punishment for juvenile
offenses, but he also looks at the capital punishment practices of the
entire world. Citing the universal movement away from the practice,
Kennedy notes that "it is fair to say that the United States now stands
alone in a world that has turned its face against the juvenile death
penalty."[1] Dissenting, Justice Scalia was outraged by the suggestion
that the United States look to other countries as a guide for penal codes.
Yet historical research into the origins of American penal practices
reveals that from the very beginning they were formed in relationship
to other countries, most specifically, in contrast to Great Britain.

Today, the United States stands apart from many countries in its sanguinary penal practices. This is a fascinating position to consider, as the
founding of the country was in part inspired by the illegitimate penal
practices of Great Britain, and early political philosophers saw leniency
in punishment as the way to characterize the United States as a compar-
atively enlightened regime. For example, the charter statement of the

Society for Political Enquiries asserted that they had "grafted on an infant commonwealth, the manners of ancient and corrupted monarchies," by adopting many of the laws of the Crown. "In having effected a separate government, we have as yet effected but a partial independence. The Revolution can only be said to be complete, when we shall have freed ourselves, no less from the influence of foreign prejudices than from the fetters of foreign power."[2] The hearings in various states over capital punishment reflected the idea that the new republic could distinguish itself and define democracy through a starkly contrasting approach to penality. While Britain's code still awarded death or transport for virtually all felonies, a few states in the new republic abolished the death penalty, and most of them severely restricted its use.

The fact that 210 years later the United States, in Kennedy's words, stood alone in the execution of juveniles shows how far we have come from that first impulse to set an example for the supposedly "enlightened" regimes of Western Europe. This lost moment of democratic idealism deserves to be resurrected as we contemplate the future of punishment in the United States. Here is one historical instance in which the character and philosophy of a country was defined in part through practices and ideals of punishment, and self-consciously so.

Most recent work on punishment emphasizes how punishment reflects and enforces particular social, political, and economic trends. I generally agree with the position articulated by, for example, Rusche and Kirschheimer that punishment often serves economic imperatives.[3] Similarly, Foucault's analysis of the growth of administrative power perceptible both in and outside the prison resonates. For those who see the use of punishment primarily being driven by politicized, economic, or institutionalist logic, the jurisprudence of the early American republic is a startling counterexample. This is not to say that this idealism is always long lasting, or strong enough to fight institutional logic that may run counter to the original intention. While the idealism may have been rapidly occluded, for a short period practitioners and philosophers tried to reconcile practices of punishment with genuine democratic fervor. We can learn more about democracy and punishment by revisiting it.

The Sanguinary Empire

One of the most pressing duties of the convention assembled to write the Pennsylvania State Constitution in 1776 was reforming the criminal code. An intensive debate about criminal law and punishment raged throughout the ex-colonies for the next twenty years, but it boiled with particular fervor in Philadelphia. The "sanguinary punishments" forced upon the state were a large point of resentment between the Quaker settlers and the Crown. In a study commissioned by the Pennsylvania Legislature, William Bradford argued that the death penalty needed to be abolished, as it was a remnant of a corrupt aristocratic regime. Allowing harsh punishment was sign that the new republic had not yet achieved full independence. "Hence sanguinary punishments, contrived in despotic and barbarous ages, have been continued when the progress of freedom, science, and morals renders them unnecessary and mischievous: and laws, the offspring of a corrupted monarchy, are fostered in the bosom of a youthful republic."[4]

The image is striking and appears repeatedly in documents from this era, as in the charter of the Society for Political Enquiries written by Thomas Paine. Law needs to be purified in order to have a truly clean foundation upon which to build American democracy. The psychology of the age was largely oedipal: there was a desire to break free from the rule of the Father, yet a terror of growing to become like him through independence. Jefferson worried about national debt and even the establishment of a permanent constitution, precisely because he did not want the mistakes or decisions of a previous generation to fetter the existence of the next: "no society can make a perpetual constitution, or even a perpetual law. The earth belongs always to the living generation."[5] What a tremendous symbol of independence: to plant a tree of moral reform and optimism in human nature that would spring forth from the ground literally watered with the blood of English and Irish convicts. Dozens of commentators argued, and the legislators in Massachusetts, Virginia, and New Hampshire agreed, that the United States should stand alone in the world, turning its face from corporal punishment of all kinds. Finding inspiration from Montesquieu and even more from the Italian Cesare Beccaria, early American philosophers and penal practitioners engaged in an extended debate about how best to create a system of punishment that would serve as an instrument of democratic morality.

When Tocqueville and Beaumont came to study the Eastern State Penitentiary (or Cherry Hill as it was then called) in 1830, these ideas had found their institutionalization in a building similar to Bentham's panopticon. Foucault's *Discipline and Punish* famously examined the birth of the prison and the ideals of the penitentiary as the development of the means of correct training—the individualism, behaviorism, and self-regulation that were required by mass democracies found their expression in schools, prisons, and the factory. While there can be no doubt that this less inspiring practice of punishment did ultimately emerge out of these institutions, research demonstrates that the initial impulse was far more idealistic. Behaviorism was explicitly rejected in favor of a more fundamental belief in human virtue.

Hence, this period of debate and penal practice between 1790 and 1810 displays a naïveté. But it also serves as a curious mirror, for many of the practices that were explicitly linked to despotism in England are now practiced in the United States. Perhaps in these foundational artic-ulations of democratic ideology we can find a position from which to critique current penal practices. Have we become the sanguinary empire from which we broke? Did institutions take on a life of their own, creating practices and effects that were not intended? Or are the ideals of punishment always bound to be nobler than the practices, cre-ating an inescapable chasm between ideals of justice and practices of power?

Transportation

Australia's origins as a penal colony are well known; America's are not. European powers had long used punishment as a way to advance colo-nial ambitions, starting with the use of galley slaves in the sixteenth century. Rusche and Kirschheimer use the example of galley servitude as a demonstration of their argument that economic considerations rather than moral ones have historically determined the nature of pun-ishment. They reprint a letter from a public prosecutor in Bordeaux to the national administration written in 1676.

> You have frequently done me the honor of writing to me in connec-tion with the supply of prisoners for the galleys and of transmitting to me the express orders of His Majesty relating to the use of such prisoners in the execution of his glorious projects. You will be grati-fied to learn that this Court has twenty prisoners who will be chained together this morning and sent off.[6]

Galley slaves were needed to power the fleets of the different crowns of Europe: 350 rowers were needed for the larger ships of the era, and 180 for the smaller ones.[7] Because of the dangerous and ghastly nature of the work, it was impossible to power the fleets with free men, so prisoners were found (some might even say, made) to do so. It is particularly vivid to realize that trade, war, and expansion were literally powered by thousands of enslaved prisoners at precisely the time that Grotius was penning "The Free Sea" providing the theoretical and legal justification for the expansion of free trade.

Technological innovation made galley slaves largely obsolete by the eighteenth century, but prisoners could be useful for the projects of empire in other ways. Settlers in Virginia asked the government to send them convicts to help with labor in 1611 but found their labor unreliable and their administration so difficult that they soon reconsidered this source of labor. In 1670 in Virginia and 1676 in Maryland, the colonists passed laws prohibiting the transport of convicts into their territory.[8] That such a measure was needed testifies to the commonality of the practice.

Eighteenth-century English penal laws were draconian. The death penalty was prescribed for virtually every felony, but jails were overcrowded nonetheless. Fewer people were convicted of crimes since the result would be death. While it might seem obvious that a reform of the penal code was required, instead in 1717 Parliament passed the Transportation Act. The act is remarkably frank about the failure of the English penal code and suggests a more productive alternative.

> Whereas it is found by Experience, That the Punishments inflicted by the Laws now in Force against the Offences of Robbery, Larceny, and other felonious Taking and Stealing of Money and Goods, have not proved effectual to deter wicked and evil-disposed Persons from being guilty of the said Crimes. . . . And whereas in many of his Majesty's Colonies and Plantations in America, there is great Want of servants, who by their Labour and Industry might be the Means of improving and making the said Colonies and plantations more useful to the nation.[9]

This act of Parliament made it possible to commute the death penalty for felonies and substitute transportation to the colonies for either seven or fourteen years as the alternative punishment. The question of whether the transport sentence was to last seven or fourteen years depended upon if the crime was classified as a "clergy crime."[10] The official rationale that colonists were anxious to receive these convicts was belied by the existence of laws in Virginia, Maryland, and Pennsylvania specifically barring the importation of convicts. The Transportation Act of 1717 made all these oppositional laws null and void, however, and the large-scale transport of convicts to America commenced.

Roger Ekrich's research provides a sketch of the practice. In the years between 1749 and 1771, 40 percent of those convicted of crimes at Old Bailey were transported into the American colonies.[11] Other research takes a longer period of focus and finds that between 1729 and 1770, 70 percent of convicts from Old Bailey were transported to the colonies. Clearly, the practice fundamentally changed criminal punishment in England as well as immigration into the colonies. Most notoriously, James Oglethorpe arranged for 16,000 debtors to be released from prison to go and settle in the newly founded colony of Georgia. In the eighteenth century, one-quarter of all immigrants from England and Ireland into the American colonies were convicts.[12]

The practice was wildly profitable, almost as much as the slave trade. Jonathan Forward was the London merchant who had a virtual monopoly on transport from 1718 until 1738.[13] The criminal justice system handed convicts over to Forward, who then loaded them into boats and shipped them to the American colonies. Upon arrival in North America, he sold the convicts to plantation owners, or any other masters, who would be able to use their labor for either seven or fourteen years depending upon their crime. Plantation owners liked to buy convicts, because they cost much less than a slave. The average cost of a slave was 50 pounds for an adult, while it was a mere 12 to 15 pounds for a convict. Because of procreation and permanent enslavement, the long-term economy of slaves may have been better. But because they were a short-term investment, convicts did not have to be treated as well. Fifty percent of convict laborers died within seven years, suggesting that they were worked to death.[14]

The reason convict labor was relatively inexpensive was that the transporters did not have to pay for their cargo as did slave traders, and they capitalized grandly upon the voyage back home as well. The government handed convicts over to the merchants for free, happy to be rid of the expense of execution or detainment. Balak and Lave closely examined the political economy of convict transportation and found that the profitability was also due to the "return cargo" such as sugar,

tobacco, and cotton that they brought back to London. This was a crucial factor in perpetuating the practice: transportation to the colonies of
Canada failed when the War of Independence made transport impossible into the United States.[15] Because there weren't as many products
available in Canada to make the return trip profitable, the transportation of convict labor across the Atlantic ceased to be a venture that
attracted London businessmen.

Hence, the transport of convicts was a lucrative business that inter-
sected well with the development of colonial products. The English
criminal system soon found that transportation was an ideal solution to
the overcrowding of jails. Between 1720 and 1765 Parliament passed
sixteen different laws making transportation the required punishment
for different crimes. This historical case study suggests that the practice
of punishment at the time was developed according to economic principles, as Rusche and Kirschheimer argue throughout their classic book
Punishment and Social Structure. From the galley slave system to transportation, one can see how England used the penal code as a way to
promote imperial ambitions.

The transportation system allowed merchants to profit from the
crime wave that accompanied industrialization in England, helped
people the colonies, provided labor for tasks that even indentured servants were loath to take on, and provided an inexpensive way for
England to rid itself of the "criminal classes" without having to kill
them off one by one. Presented with a choice of execution or exile, convicts found little to resent in transportation. The only people who were
less than enthusiastic about the entire system were the colonial administrators who complained about the disorder caused by transportation.
They aptly perceived that they were bearing most of the unfortunate
outcomes of this ingenious system of justice. Since they could no longer
bar transport outright following the 1717 Transportation Act, instead
they sought ways to regulate and curb it. They tried both taxation and
red tape to strangle the practice. Some states required intensive regis-
tration procedures for transporters to be eligible to sell convicts. Others
placed taxation per head on each convict sold, attempting to tip the economics that made the practice so profitable.[16]

However, the Crown was so supportive of the policy that soon transporters recognized that they could ignore the colonial administrators
with impunity. The Crown wouldn't enforce these taxes or regulations,
so transporters saw no need to pay them. This is but one place where

the sovereignty of the Crown was asserted over the colonies. However, this clash over transportation produced an interesting response in the colonies, and later the newly independent United States. The colonies, having played an integral role in bolstering a corrupt system of justice for many decades, were all the more eager to establish their moral superiority by establishing a code of punishment that served democratic ideals, rather than aristocratic corruption.

Intransigent in many things, England continued to try to ship convicts to the United States even after independence. In 1787, the Continental Congress passed a resolution urging all states to ban the transport of convicts from Britain as soon as possible. In Britain, the sudden closing of their primary release valve for the criminal justice system caused crisis and soul-searching. In 1779, Britain passed a resolution calling for transportation to resume elsewhere. When transport to Canada proved to be unfeasible for economic reasons, Lord Beauchamp was appointed to prepare reports examining the possibility of transport to other regions. In a report to Parliament in 1785 entitled "Recommendations for the Disposal of Convicts," Beauchamp noted the overcrowding of jails, which were bursting with prisoners who had been sentenced to transportation many years earlier but had not been able to be transported due to the American Revolution. Beauchamp suggests that transportation has the disadvantage of not providing the example to discourage future crime, since "his Sufferings are unseen. . . . His Chasm is soon filled up, and, being as soon forgotten, it strikes no Terror into the Minds of those for whose Correction it was intended to operate, though the Public may gain very importantly by his Removal." Nonetheless, the Lord recommends a coast of Africa (present day Namibia), which has a favorable climate and "A vein of Copper Ore which contains one third of pure metal," and furthermore would be an excellent stopping place for those returning to England from India. To establish the colony, the Lord suggests they land convicts in November as "they will have the whole Summer to raise Habitations, and make other preparations for their future Subsistence and Security." Happily, the administration of these convicts can be accomplished by loyalists from America who "are desirous of settling in any healthy Part of the Globe where they can rely upon the protection of the British Government."[17] Ideally, the colony would flourish and become the destination for all transportation and emigrants from England.[18] They hoped to provide ample economic opportunities for British subjects to remain under the protection of the Crown, rather than being tempted to go to the United States.

New South Wales, Australia, became the location of choice instead, due to the fact that Namibia was considered "sandy and barren, and from other causes unfit for settlement," but the logic behind the argument for Namibia is revealing nonetheless.[19] One can see the colonial administration at work, trying to gain "The greatest national Advantages" from the system of criminal justice.

There were dissenters in the empire itself, the most well known to us today being Jeremy Bentham. In 1802 he wrote a long pamphlet arguing that Parliament should abandon the system of transportation to New South Wales in favor of expanding the penitentiary system of his device, the panopticon. In this pamphlet, Bentham proposes five criteria by which to measure the effectiveness of punishment: deterrence, reformation, incapacitation, compensation (satisfaction to the injured party), and economy. Interestingly enough, Bentham argues that the transportation system to American was effective, as the prevalence of law-abiding citizens and the purchase of convicts by one particular master who was to train the convict in the manners and habits of society fulfilled the need to have punishment serve as a transformative process. Yet transport to New South Wales accomplished no similar transformation, as the colony was overrun by convicts with no positive influence to offer one another. In his eyes, even more damaging is the fact that transport is not perfectly proportional to the crime committed, breaking one of his cardinal rules. Furthermore, sentences were frequently commuted, and those with means could buy their own way out of the servitude that was required of them. Therefore mere banishment became the punishment for the wealthy, while banishment combined with bondage became the fate of the poor, even though they had received the same sentence. Frequently convicts escaped and returned to Britain. Bentham argues that even though the system may be profitable, the price is too high to pay: "The price, in the way of injustice—the whole price is thus paid for the expected benefit; and it is but in an imperfect degree that the benefit is reaped. The proportions of penal justice are confounded; the poison of perfidy is infused into the system of government; and still the obnoxious vermin remain unextirpated."[20]

Bentham offers his penitentiary system as the favorable alternative, one that will serve the interests of justice rather than the purse. He proposes to see convicts as a "sort of grown children" that need the same basic guidance as other children to attain the means of self-legislation. The penitentiary is perfectly poised to accomplish this task, "in its extraordinary and improved state, that principle of management carried to such a degree of perfection, as till then had never been reached even by imagination, much less by practice."[21] Bentham argues that the penitentiary system is superior to transport on every criterion except for economy. He clearly hopes that the advantages in terms of justice will persuade Parliament that the extra expense is justified. In the fifteen years following the breakdown of the transport system to the United States, Britain was involved in a period of self-scrutiny and had delegations report on the penal practices of the United States as a model to consider for adoption. Interestingly, Bentham felt compelled to send this particular pamphlet to a sympathetic fellow traveler in the United States, Caleb Lownes.[22] Lownes was the administrator of the Walnut Street Jail in Philadelphia. On the face of it, he may seem to be similarly inspired by Bentham's vision, but closer inspection reveals that the initial penal philosophies and practices in Philadelphia were derived from a different source and have a distinct character.

Beccaria

Bernard Bailyn has noted that Cesare Beccaria's work was mentioned in pamphlet after pamphlet about criminal law in the new republic. John Adams, Thomas Jefferson, Thomas Paine, and Benjamin Franklin were all well acquainted with the work *On Crimes and Punishments.* It was published in Italy in 1764, and the English translation of the work was remarkably swift, appearing in 1767. Presses in the colonies reprinted it as early as 1773, and multiple editions appeared in South Carolina, New York, Boston, and Pennsylvania.[23] First editions of the Italian work appear in the American Philosophical Library in Philadelphia, as well as multiple copies of these eighteenth-century American editions. Beccaria is hailed as "wise," "immortal," and even saintly in different treatises immediately following the Revolutionary War.

Though Beccaria is often seen merely as a short detour on the way to Bentham, their ideas are actually quite distinct.[24] While the utilitarianism of Bentham may have finally triumphed in the practices of the penitentiary described by Tocqueville, Beaumont, and Foucault, Beccaria served as the initial inspiration behind the development of a new penal idealism. In Beccaria we find a unique vision of the utility of law in creating democratic virtue and citizens, an insight into the psychology of democratic nations that compares to Tocqueville's, and a vision of how democratic virtue, not merely behavior, can be created through public policy. Ultimately, Beccaria's work suggests why punishment is so dangerous in a democratic society, but it also offers suggestions for how it can be used to create equality.

One theme in Beccaria's work that found favor among the new legislators in the United States was the idea that bad laws are the source of criminality. This is different from claiming that laws are bad because they do not prevent criminality. On the contrary, poor laws produce criminality. They asserted that the criminals Britain had sent over to the American colonies were an effect of corrupt laws. People are not the source of criminality; rather, poor government is. The corollary to this proposition is that good laws can be a fount of virtue. Beccaria claimed that any law that goes against human sentiment would ultimately meet resistance. The surest way of generating resistance is to force adherence to a law that people find naturally abhorrent. On the other hand, making punishment perfectly just will create a sovereign that will never need to be overthrown. In this sense, punishment becomes the calibration between government and the people—the more closely the government matches what is in the human heart, the more likely that this government will never be deposed. Correct punishment becomes a way to ensure perpetuity of law, or even the end of all revolutions. This idea would have obvious appeal in a country seeking to establish a stable regime. But stability could not come at any price—for example, compelling obedience to a regime—at least, not at this historical juncture. Correct law was the way to achieve stability without sacrificing progress.

Beccaria extends this basic observation throughout his discussion of crime and punishment. What he seems to fear above all is the observation of laws, without a concurrent belief in their justice. He takes the highly unusual step of imagining what people who are being subjected to the law must think when they see that the law is applied irregularly or believe that the law is unjust. Both Beccaria and the political thinkers of the early American republic had seen quite clearly how English law was used as an instrument to increase the fortunes of the ruling classes. For colonists who had tried to resist transport, they had experienced the penal system as a clear affront to their ability to self-legislate. Because they had experienced firsthand how punishment can be a tool that reflects and increases social inequalities, they recognized the need to guard vigilantly against this use of the criminal codes.

When a person, group, or entire population is forced to submit to laws that they recognize as unjust, the essence of the social contract is destroyed. Obedience to law without believing in the law only creates resentment, not the social cohesion that is intended. Beccaria acknowledges that punishment in a stratified society only leads to further disassociation from the state and justice. He imagines the calculations of someone facing the death penalty: "these laws are nothing but pretexts for power and for the calculated and cruel formalities of justice; they are nothing but a convenient language for killing us all the more surely, like the preselected victims of a sacrifice to the insatiable god of despotism."[25] Forcing blind obedience is the way to foment revolt, to undermine the political order entirely. Just as the son waits for the first opportunity to overthrow the tyrannical father, so punishments that create compliance but appear to be unjust are the most volatile element in the relationship between state and citizen. Beccaria's own relationship with his father has been documented as a particularly troubled one; who better to ruminate on the resentment caused by feigned obedience?[26]

This is the aspect of Beccaria's thought that most clearly separates him from Bentham. Bentham argued punishment should serve social cohesion and be gauged to be maximally useful in preventing future crimes. But Beccaria sees the origin of social cohesion as resting in the contract; therefore punishment must serve to enforce the contract, not simply social cohesion. Obtaining correct behavior through punishment without true acceptance of the society and government opens the road to revolt. Beccaria's tract contains a short précis on education. His ideas about education display exactly how distant he is from the "Means of Correct Training" at work in both prisons and schools described by Foucault in *Discipline and Punish*. Education should "replace copies with originals" in the minds of students and eschew "ordering them what to do, which gains only a feigned and fleeting obedience."[27] Learning happens when students think for themselves; they should not be encouraged to repeat the knowledge of others. Beccaria correctly foresaw that behaviorism would undermine the spirit of contractual government.

Punishment is useful in preventing future crime, but the principle of utility cannot be the guide in developing it. Instead, Beccaria asserts that the proper way to determine a punishment is by the effect it has upon those administering and witnessing it. "The limit which the law-giver should set to the harshness of punishments seems to depend on when the feeling of compassion at the punishment, meant more for the spectators than for the convict, begins to dominate every other in their souls."[28] What is the punishment that brings out compassion? This seems to depend more upon the response of the person being punished than the actual punishment. Take, for example, sending a child to his or her room. If the child sorrowfully and dutifully goes to the room, stifling cries, and sits inside quietly moaning, compassion is felt much more easily than if the child resists, screams, and slams the bedroom door after yelling at you. The punishment is the same, but in one instance it seems harsh, in the other, perhaps too lenient.

Another factor that determines the level of compassion in spectators is whether the punishment itself corresponds to what they feel is correct. If we gather in public to watch a hand be slapped for an aggravated assault, we would have no compassion for the convict; instead we would only marvel or feel outrage at his luck in escaping something more severe. On the other hand, when punishments are harsher than seem appropriate, two events are likely to occur. First, we think the law is unjust and distance ourselves from it—it is the law of the regime, not the law of the social contract of which I am a part. But spectators will also be more likely to refuse identification with the person being punished. To convince oneself of safety even in the midst of an unjust law, we reason that the condemned must be of an entirely different sort of person than myself. There would be no empathy and hence no compassion. Beccaria argues against the public punishment of smugglers. "Smuggling is a real crime against the sovereign and the nation, but the punishment of it should not involve dishonour since it does not seem disgraceful in the eyes of the public. If humiliating punishments are given to crimes not held to be dishonourable, then the feeling of disgrace aroused by those that really are so diminishes." Instead of seeing the law as a reflection of innate human sensibility, it seems to be an instrument of humiliation, and "the moral sentiments are destroyed."[29]

The basic insight is interesting, as Beccaria observes that punishment can create a chasm in societies by developing a class that becomes untouchable, an entire category of people that we come to see as less than human as a result of their punishment. It is when punishments create different classes of citizens that they fail to reflect the unity of the social body through contract but instead perpetuate the division. Once punishment serves to divide, all hope of justice is gone as the contract and law must be based upon unity. This idea of unity was to guide many practices of the Walnut Street Jail in Philadelphia, as I will discuss shortly.

Beccaria laments the uneven application of the laws to different social classes as well as the use of punishment in creating a permanent social schism. Once again, he puts himself into the head of a criminal being tried.

> What are these laws which I have to obey, which leave such a gulf between me and the rich man? He denies me the penny I beg of him, brushing me off with the demand that I should work, something he knows nothing about. Who made these laws? Rich and powerful men, who have never condescended to visit the filthy hovels of the poor, who have never broken mouldy bread among the innocent cries of starving children and a wife's tears. Let us break these ties, which are pernicious to most people and only useful to a few and idle tyrants; let us attack injustice at its source. . . . King of a small band of men, I shall put to rights the inequities of fortune, and I shall see these tyrants blanch and cower at one whom they considered, with insulting ostentation, lower than their horses and dogs.[30]

It may sound like *ressentiment*, but it is a jarring passage to find in the midst of an otherwise straightforward plea for the proper structuring of law in the purpose of punishing. In these passages, he strikes at the core of the problem of democracy and punishment: when we punish, we make someone less than ourselves. The paradox of punishment in a democracy is that punishment is ideally used to encourage and demand that someone act as one of the self-legislating individuals that form the basis of an equal society. Yet the very act of punishing makes someone inherently *less* than those others in the position of enforcing the contract. Today, most people accept the idea that once someone breaks the law, they fall outside of normal citizenship. Once a sentence is served, a fine paid, the offender is supposedly to be welcomed back into society. Yet Beccaria's work helps remind us why that is so difficult. The process of punishing makes someone less than equal, and the stigma remains. We cannot place someone in a prison and outside of society according to a time regulation and expect their reentry into society to be seamless. Punishment can only work to promote democracy if it is circumscribed to very precise effect.

Beccaria saw the problem and tried to calculate a form of punishment that would maintain democratic citizenship. He concludes it is crucial for compassion to be maintained on the side of the onlooker, whether a passive observer of punishment or someone involved in the actual administration of it. He also insists that understanding must be established in the mind of the person being punished. If punishment is to maintain a democratic society, it must not break the bounds of natural compassion among fellow citizens, nor can it create the perception of privilege among different classes.

Beccaria's vision of punishment would not work in a society where there were different classes, for any criminal would then be able to blame his inequality for his penance. If there are already classes in society, practices of punishment will reveal the inequity starkly. Beccaria's work suggests why punishment and criminal codes must be reformed if democracy is to flourish. What had been the instrument of inequality must be wrested away, lest it corrupt the heart of the new republic. We might look at this idea today and say that such ideals are noble, but that the practice of punishment will inevitably create some sort of hierarchy between judge and defendant, guard and prisoner. Yet the practices of the Walnut Street Jail in Philadelphia in the years immediately following the American Revolution were closely aligned with Beccaria's ideas. They did try to create compassion between keeper and prisoner, and the goal of the system was to maintain every person's identity as a full citizen, even while they were in prison.

Democratic Punishment: The Practices at Walnut Street Jail, 1790–99

The Walnut Street Jail in Philadelphia was the first experiment in democratic punishment, and this is where the idea of the penitentiary was initially developed.[31] Settlers built the Walnut Street Jail in 1773. In 1777, the British army seized Philadelphia and used the jail to house prisoners of war. The notoriously cruel Captain Cunningham was charged with the administration of the jail and the rebel prisoners within it. When he was finally charged with numerous crimes in London in 1791, Cunningham confessed that he had "presided over the miseries of over two thousand prisoners in the New York and Philadelphia Provosts; how he had stopped the rations of his victims and sold them for his own gain." A report on the jail holding colonial prisoners stated of Cunningham: "His chief amusement, when not in a sanguinary mood, was to defeat the benevolent intention of the people of the city who sent in food to the patriotic prisoners, by upsetting the utensils and scattering the food over the filthy floor. He would chuckle to witness the degrading scramble of the poor wretches as they gathered it up, dirt and all, to mitigate the pangs of starvation."[32] On average ten people a day died in the jail, and their bodies were unceremoniously dragged across the street and dumped in ditches in a field in the middle of Philadelphia.[33] Transforming the clear symbol of British malevolence was a victory for the administrators of the jail following independence.

In 1776, the new Constitution of Pennsylvania replaced the Code of the Duke of York, which had been foisted onto the colony in 1718, bringing the bloody criminal code of native England to Penn's territory. William Penn had successfully resisted this criminal code and had established a much more lenient and progressive penal code in 1682 under the name of "The Great Law." With the Transportation Act of 1717, however, the Crown was no longer going to allow colonies to have a criminal code separate from, and often in resistance to, its own. William Bradford noted that the criminal codes of much of the eighteenth century in Pennsylvania were "an exotic plant, and not the native growth of Pennsylvania. It has endured, but, I believe, has never been a favorite. As soon as the principles of Beccaria were disseminated, they found a soil that was prepared to receive them."[34]

Thus, one of the first significant shifts from British law was the Pennsylvania penal code.

> To deter more effectually from the commission of crimes, by continued visible punishment of long duration, and to make sanguinary punishment less necessary; houses ought to be provided for punishing at hard labor, those who shall be convicted of crimes not capital; wherein the criminals shall be employed for the benefit of the public, or for reparation of injuries done to private persons. And all persons at proper times shall be admitted to see the prisoners at their labour.[35]

It is important to recall that this was considered a great improvement in the penal codes, though the resulting practices were unsavory.

In fact, the Wheel Barrow Laws, as they came to be known, are remarkably similar to the description of punishment that appears in Sir
Thomas More's *Utopia*. In Utopia, all people convicted of crimes
became slaves to the state, doing public works and generally providing
the difficult labor absolutely necessary for the maintenance of any society. The slaves are well treated, and the public display of their labor
serves as a constant reminder that one must contribute to the collective
endeavors of the commonwealth or become a slave to them absolutely.

In Philadelphia, prisoners working in public were shackled to a ball
and chain and were subjected to taunts and abuses. The convicts fought
back. "After they had swept around them as far as the ball and chain
would permit, the manacled prisoners would pick up the balls and
carry them to a fresh spot. The more malicious would often throw
down the balls in such a manner as to injure passers-by."[36] There were
several well-publicized escapes as well. On May 8, 1787, the Philadelphia Society for Alleviating the Miseries of Public Prisons was founded,
and it still exists today under the name of the Philadelphia Prison Society. One of the founders, Benjamin Rush, presented a paper against the
practice of public punishments at Franklin's salon, The Society for
Political Enquiry. Rush's primary rationale against public punishment
was that it created a permanent stigma attached to the criminal. Thus,
the practice of punishment ultimately does more to break the harmony
of society than the initial crime. "Crimes produce a stain, which may be
washed out by reformation, and which frequently wears away by time;
But public punishments leave scars, which disfigure the whole character; and hence persons, who have suffered them, are even afterwards
viewed with horror or aversion."[37] After several months of lobbying on
the part of Rush and the rest of the Philadelphia Society, the Wheel Barrow Laws were repealed on April 5, 1790. Private labor was established
as an alternative to the public spectacle of hard labor. The Walnut Street
Jail was to be the primary location for this private labor.

The administration of the Walnut Street Jail was turned over to the
Philadelphia Society for Alleviating the Miseries of Public Prisons, and
Caleb Lownes, member of that society, became the primary administrator and designer of the jail, though there were other volunteer
observers who met twice monthly to observe the workings at the jail
and discuss reformation. There are two different detailed accounts of
the workings of the Walnut Street Jail in the following years. Lownes
himself wrote one in 1793, which was attached to William Bradford's

proposal to end capital punishment in Pennsylvania. Robert Turnbull in 1796, a South Carolina native who was studying law in Philadelphia when he toured the jail, wrote the second. He later became a political reformer in the South. Both Turnbull and Lownes cite the ideas of Beccaria with particular favor.

Turnbull is an enthusiast for the system, describing the jail as the "wonder of the world." At this time, the jail held 250 convicts, who were segregated by sex. Everyone worked in the common yard of the jail and then retired to their individual cells to sleep. They ate meals in common. On Sundays ministers visited the jail, and there was some literacy instruction as well. The characteristics that distinguish the entire enterprise are the relationship between the keepers and the prisoners, the method of punishment, and the attitude toward criminality.

Lownes chastised those who "forget that the prisoner is a rational being of like feelings and passion with themselves." While Bentham was to later describe convicts and prisoners in the penitentiary system as children needing instruction, this view was not held at the Walnut Street Jail. Crimes were not understood as a result of individual moral or rational failings. Instead, Turnbull observes, "you attribute their situation to misfortune, to bad education, and other adventitious circumstances in life—not to any innate thirst for vice or villainy."[38] Every pain was taken to create a bond between rather than segregate the keepers of the jail and the prisoners. The companionship between the two was seen as an essential element in their reformation, as emulation rather than training or discipline was seen as the core of the prisoners' transformation. Prisoners need to have a reason to emulate the guards, and therefore their manners must be irreproachable. Corporal discipline would destroy the desire of the prisoner to identify with the keeper and was therefore completely forbidden. In a reversal of contemporary beliefs, Turnbull acknowledges the necessity of corporal discipline for a child who does not have a fully developed rational capability, while he spurns it for the convict. "With children or boys, no other principle than that of fear will govern, and perhaps no punishment avail more than whipping; but where reflection once holds a post in the mind, I have been always firmly persuaded, that mankind would more likely be reformed by almost any other mode."[39]

When Turnbull visited the jail, there were 250 prisoners who were administered by four guards and one female warden, none of who had weapons of any sort. Solitary confinement was administered to those who refused to work or upset the order and harmony of the jail in any way. While Eastern State Penitentiary was to take solitary confinement as the fundamental experience of penance, here it was a form of discipline, not of complete reform. Interestingly, the goal of solitary confinement was to make the prisoner realize the power of his rationale, his mental capabilities. Solitary confinement might be understood as taking the presumed virtues of democratic individualism to its logical conclusion. Individuals, not society, are rational and moral. Therefore, removing the individual from all social intercourse will allow this individualism to blossom once more in its full promise. Benjamin Rush believed that the soul could recalibrate itself once removed from the overstimulus of modern sociability. On the other hand, there is an awareness of the psychological underpinnings of the experience revealed by the description provided by Turnbull.

> We become by it gradually acquainted with a true knowledge of ourselves; with the purity of dictates prescribed to us by our consciences; and of course easier convinced of the necessity of conforming to them. It is in this state of seclusion from the world that the mind can be brought to contemplate itself—to judge of its powers—and thence to acquire the resolution and energy necessary to protect its avenues from the intrusion of vicious thoughts.[40]

Solitary confinement is where one can come to see that the mind can be one's most terrible enemy. It forces inmates to achieve mental discipline in a way similar to meditation if they are to survive intact.

Keepers were more than guards or bureaucrats. They were allowed to commute sentences when they thought that they saw true reformation in a prisoner. As opposed to the impartial administrators of Lockean liberalism, guards were encouraged to socialize and converse with the prisoners in order to gauge the convicts' progress. Turnbull recounts a discussion between a woman inmate and an inspector for the prison. She asks the inspector if her sentence might be commuted, and they discuss the matter for some time. When he concludes that as she has not served half of her sentence, it would be impossible, she reportedly "resumed her spinning with cheerfulness ... perfectly satisfied with his reasoning." Given the context, it is tempting to conclude that the cheerfulness was artifice. However, Turnbull also recounts that convicts happily greeted one of the keepers who had been ill for a week and away from the jail. Even the appearance, if not heartfelt sincerity, of such a sentiment is inconceivable today.

Lest we think that Turnbull was an overzealous enthusiast and Lownes a bureaucrat serving his own interest, we find other testimony to the spirit behind the jail. In 1798, an anonymous "Lady" wrote the following ode, "The Pennsylvania Prison," that was published in the *Philadelphia Monthly Magazine.*

It is a sort of little commonwealth (if I may be allowed the expression) which I shall entitle the commonwealth of nature—an excellent school to teach the utility of that government, which attends most to its operations, to the uniformity, beauty, and simplicity of her divine precepts,—health and contentment must exist, where wisdom and humanity reign, and the breast of the most hardened convict, will naturally admit contrition, and embrace reformation, while experiencing the bodily comfort, the mental satisfaction, and pecuniary benefit, that lead to, and is the foundation of them,—virtue *will* display her charms, to beings who never before beheld her, and they will instinctively be led to adore and follow what has afforded so much tranquil, solid pleasure—in pursuing industry and good order, they will *see* is the only roads that leads to happiness, while idleness, and its concomitant vice, they will feel, leads only to misery.—The Philadelphia prison, is one of the most striking emblems, of *progress* in refinement.[41]

The prison was seen as a microcosm of government, rather than a deviation from it. The prisoner was encouraged to see himself or herself as part of society, rather than apart from it. Inherent in the administration of the jail then was the goal of preventing a hierarchy developing between prisoner and administrator.

Yet this experiment was to last for only nine years. Thomas Dumm has brilliantly detailed the quick evolution toward the more behaviorist impulse in American penal theory in his book *Democracy and Punishment.* The change from the desire to reform to the goal of creating obedience is best captured by Tocqueville and Beaumont's observations about the distinction between the Pennsylvania Model of Penitentiary and the Auburn Model. The Pennsylvania system made labor within solitary confinement its primary method of reform. In every cell in Eastern State penitentiary, there is a gap in the ceiling called "the eye of God." Every day the sun passed slowly over the cell, and the prisoner was to engage in an extended self-study, under the all-knowing eye of God. In Auburn, prisoners worked collectively, though in complete silence. The combination of collective work and silence displayed the virtues of sociality and obedience. Prisoners saw the benefits of collective endeavor, without speaking and contaminating each other's thoughts. The obedience required to be silent in a room full of other prisoners was much different than the ability to remain sane after seeing no one for an extended period of time. Tocqueville and Beaumont summarized the differences between the two systems as following: the Pennsylvania system produces more virtuous citizens, while the Auburn model produces more obedient ones.

Maybe the Walnut Street system was simply unsustainable because an institutional logic became more prominent as the founding ideas faded. Who is to remember the blueprint when the actual construction of a place deviates from it? The cost of the Pennsylvania system was also quite high. In fact the British government placed financial concerns over all others when choosing transportation to South Wales rather than Bentham's penitentiary. One other factor seems worth consideration. The existence of penal labor may have made the system too susceptible to appropriation by private interests, an issue that will be more fully explored in chapter 6, "Hitched to the Post: Prison Labor, Choice, and Citizenship." More likely, behaviorism and utilitarianism were much less difficult goals to achieve than moral reformation. The fervor of democratic sentiment faded, and the realities of creating democratic order grew more apparent.

In the end, the penitentiaries decided that the souls of prisoners could remain their own, as long as they were willing to obey their masters. Yet this is exactly what Beccaria and the founding fathers saw as the birth of tyranny as well as the betrayal of the social contract. As soon as the democratic society can be divided between those who believe in the rectitude of the code of law and those who are subject to it, law and society appears as a sham, an instrument. It is ironic that we have misread Beccaria for so long as a utilitarian, because he provides some of the most powerful arguments against the utilitarian version of punishment. Punishment will only be useful when it remains true to the ideal of the social contract—equally applied, transparent, and for the interest of self-regulation. Oddly, after reading Beccaria, we can see virtuous punishment as one of the pillars of a truly democratic society.

Beccaria realized that punishment could corrupt our perception and experience of the law, meaning that it is crucial to get the system right.

This does seem very idealistic, and some might claim that no person ever being punished would view their fate as deserved or legitimate without being lost in a blizzard of confusion or self-hatred. But every one of us has been punished in one way or another and recognized that we deserved it. When a person is pulled over for running a red light, she may hate to pay the fine but recognizes the need for traffic regulations and the penalties that accompany them. It is when the driver finds out that her friend was caught running a red light and did not receive the same penalty that indignation might arise. When the rule, law, or system appears as unjust, the punishment has a purely performative or tyrannical meaning. Similarly, when a punishment is clearly illogical or disproportionate, those who enforce it lose their authority and become tyrants instead, people who have power based upon coercion rather than as a result of perceived, legitimate means.

Every government needs a system of laws and a way to administer punishment. The challenge of democracy is to prevent the government and the penal system from creating a hierarchy among what should be equal citizens. Beccaria laid out the framework and rationale clearly. The moment serves as a sober reminder; perhaps the true test of whether a state can truly be considered democratic is if those sitting in the jails believe it is so. The most illuminating moments of Beccaria's text are the juxtaposition of principles of right and justice with the cynical, angry thoughts of those subject to the law. The penetrating anger of the offender makes the principles of justice seem a sham, or at least hopelessly abstract in comparison. How many prisoners in the United States today believe the laws are a manifestation of the social contract of which they are a part? How many citizens, when hearing of atrocities in prisons, feel proud or even comfortable in acknowledging that they have legislated these punishments as an equal member of the social contract? It isn't that criminality threatens our democracy; instead our punishments reveal how completely democratic idealism has disappeared.

CHAPTER 5

Punishment in Liberal Regimes

"To prove fiction, indeed," said I, "there is need of fiction; but it is characteristic of truth to need no proof but truth."
—Jeremy Bentham, *A Fragment on Government*

In a virtually manic departure from the foundations of early American democracy explored in the last chapter, today the United States incarcerates a much higher proportion of its population than any other advanced democracy. In 2003 Bruce Western measured a penal population of 2.1 million inmates, indicating a scale of incarceration that "exceeds the historic average by a factor of nearly five" in the history of the United States.[1] Analysts have measured and examined crime rates, public insecurity, shifts in (or manipulations of, depending on one's perspective) perceptions of crime, sentencing practices, institutional trajectories, and economic and racial elements to explain the punitiveness that characterizes the United States today.[2] No doubt all of these factors need to be considered. But what I offer here is another element that does not usually appear in discussions about contemporary penal practices in the United States: classical liberal political philosophy. In this chapter, I demonstrate the unique reliance upon punishment in liberal contract theory, relating it back to the role that punishment plays in the presentation and legitimation of political order. One of the most striking aspects of the current incarceration boom is how it appears to completely defy logic or utility. At great human and capital costs, we cycle an increasing percentage of the American citizenry through jails and prisons, producing little reform and a questionable impact on the crime rate. Clearly, we are pursuing this policy for reasons that are not immediately apparent. Understanding the unique reliance of liberal social contract theory on punishment to establish its terms and principles helps to explain the function of penal practices in the political order of the United States in different terms.

On the face of it, the incarceration boom in the United States seems to contradict the classical liberal tenets that venerate individual rights as much as limits upon state power. Should we see punishment and penal policy as the exception to this rule? On the contrary, when we examine the philosophies of John Locke, we find that punishment plays an integral role in defining and developing—and importantly, presenting—both individual rights and limited state power. While I do not offer liberal thought as a primary reason for contemporary incarceral policies, understanding the centrality of punishment in classical liberalism helps us to understand in part how a punitiveness that seemingly contradicts all other governmental trends is not generally viewed as problematic.

Let me conclude this introduction by clarifying what I am not arguing. It is relatively clear to argue that modern forms of penality have been instrumental in molding the kinds of behaviors desired by capitalistic, liberal regimes. The calibration between systems of punishment and the ideal political subject was explored to great effect by Foucault in *Discipline and Punish* and Thomas Dumm in *Democracy and Punishment*. I am not out to contest these arguments but rather to point out the relatively exceptional reliance upon punishment in the formation of John Locke's liberal political philosophies. He relied upon punishment to signify and represent the most basic definitions and conditions of liberal social contract theory, such as responsibility, personhood, and limited executive power.

It is simple to say that punishment is necessary to enforce the terms of the liberal social contract. Yet this would not distinguish social contract theory from any other form of government. I argue that where liberalism comes to rely uniquely upon punishment is in establishing its comparative strengths: a veneration for individual rights and circumscribed state power. How can the exercise of state power be visibly and convincingly registered as limited? How are such abstract notions as "individualism" and "responsibility" to gain meaning? In both cases, theorists turn to punishment as a way to put together the necessary elements of the liberal regime. Social contract theory claims that it is derived directly from natural rights, but a close examination of Locke demonstrates that he used punishment as the midwife in the birth of the social contract. Punishment is not an exception to the rules of liberalism, but an integral element in the classical liberal paradigm.

Punishment and the Contract

Proponents of the social contract point to the great strengths of using the metaphor of contract to structure government such as the necessary reciprocity between citizen and state, the consent that makes it possible to reconcile order to freedom, the explicit rights for individuals and limitations upon the government, and the ability to agree upon what conditions will render the contract null and void. Critics point to the contract as a scrim, a facade of consent that serves as a cover for coercion, and argue that the mechanism of the contract renders a society composed of agents and objects, exchange, rationality and calculation, as opposed to community, emotion, and love. Contract as a metaphor for organization also occludes power dynamics. Both critics and proponents take the intangibility of the contract as a given and see that its neat character stands in contrast to the messiness of social dynamics. Depending on one's point of view, this distinction can mean that contract is normative in modeling interactions and seeking to regulate them. Conversely, it can be argued that contract serves as a blinder to actual people, ambiguities, and coercion. In both views, contract is something that stands outside of the world, and hence orders it—to good or ill.

Contract may be the most powerful tool of political order to emerge since deism precisely because of its abstract existence. Empirical methods of political organization and regulation are relatively vulnerable. Institutions can be corrupt and recognized as such. Rulers can die, go mad, or produce idiotic offspring, and laws can be critiqued as written or applied. Even actual contracts contain loopholes and weaknesses that make them less than ironclad. Since no one has ever seen a social contract, much less signed one, it is difficult to point out exactly how it fails to manifest itself. Critics say as an abstraction it is a poor representation of the much messier world. Proponents point out that its remove from the everyday struggles and prejudices of life make it able to mediate fairly. How exactly does such an abstraction come to order society and state? Even God had his miracles, revelations, and spokespersons. While faith was considered all the stronger because it eschewed the need for evidence, belief in contract relies upon a similar type of devotion without the support of institutionalized faith. Contract, improbably, becomes the abstraction upon which a positivistic political order is based.

It is an indication of the power of the contract metaphor that we live in a properly contractual society today. A contract gave birth to the government that protects against abuse of contracts between individuals. A marker of our freedom as individuals is our ability to make contracts, yet the contracts themselves are what help define us as individuals. We became citizens through entering into the social contract, and contract creates our protections as citizens. There is a truly remarkable convergence in our conceptions of agency, freedom, government, and economy around the idea of contract. But this makes it virtually impossible to understand what the contract is, how it functions, where it came from, and what its effects are.

Most literature surrounding social contract theory and practices of punishment tries to justify or challenge the state's right to punish, which can and often does take away the inalienable rights upon which the social contract is based. This is a genuine problem: how can a state founded upon the sanctity of individual rights be allowed to take them away? Some have argued that crime tips the natural balance between the rights of individuals in the favor of the offender; the state must punish in order to restore the equilibrium.[3] Others have argued that membership in the social contract is predicated upon the understanding that the state will enforce laws, thereby one has already consented to one's own punishment in the case of an infraction. The consent implied in membership reconciles this curtailing of rights with individual freedom.[4] Others embrace utilitarianism, proposing that the state must punish in order to protect the rights of others in the future and that punishment should be viewed for what it produces, as opposed to how or why it achieves this goal. Others have argued that as soon as one breaks the law, that person falls out of the social contract into a state of war and thereby loses all claims to individual rights.[5]

These positions take the social contract form of government as a given and recognize the problem that punishment poses for it theoretically.[6] I think that the more interesting question is why punishment plays such a central role in the foundations of social contract theory. Since punishment places a strain upon the conception of individual rights and social contract, why does it play such a large role in their articulation?

I had long thought that the practices of liberal regimes and the theories of liberalism were incompatible—perhaps, even worse, that the ideals themselves might be complicit in the bloody practices done in their name, agreeing with others such as Pateman, Pitts, and Mehta.[7] This is why I find it particularly interesting to consider the appearance of punishment in John Locke and Jeremy Bentham—two classic variants of the liberal argument in which punishment plays a central role. I couldn't point to violence as a way to belie the claims of philosophical liberalism, because I found a stream of blood running right through the core of the liberal canon.

The Second Treatise of Government

On its most basic level, Locke's version of the social contract is an agreement between individuals or persons consenting to be bound by the rule of law. Fascinatingly, all elements of this configuration—personhood, law, rights, and contract—are defined in reference to punishment. Following Locke's own logic that individuals are the point of departure for social and legal organization, we should begin by examining personhood. While personhood is not extensively defined in *The Second Treatise of Government,* he does dwell upon the subject in *An Essay Concerning Human Understanding.* Locke asserts that personhood is a matter of consciousness. After all, I could define myself by saying I am a Philadelphian. Would I then cease to be me if I moved? I could say I am the person that occupies this body. But bodies change. Isn't the woman the same person—even though changed—as the girl who came before? What makes a person, according to Locke, is the consciousness that can connect experiences throughout time and space: "This personality extends itself beyond present existence to what is past, only by consciousness,—whereby it becomes concerned and accountable; owns and imputes to itself past actions, just upon the same ground and for the same reason as it does the present."[8] Notice that the term *accountable* rests at the center of this definition. Consciousness is what provides accountability: if I could not remember what I did yesterday or if I was reborn every day (a strangely common theme in films these days), human consciousness as is typically understood could not exist. We would have no sense of where we were, where we had been, that our actions and choices have effects, or that we are distinct from our environment.

Consciousness defines a person; it also makes every person accountable. "In this personal identity is founded all the right and justice of reward and punishment."[9] To elaborate upon this claim, he turns to punishment that, in this case, is not a system of laws and application but rather an external recognition of personhood and accountability, or the mitigation thereof. Punishment is one way our personhood is recognized by others, and the way society as a whole establishes who counts as a person and who does not. As accountability is the marker of

personality, the determination whether someone can be held accountable for his actions signals his personhood or lack thereof.

Locke's definition of personhood serves an instrumental role in his
political system. If people cannot be held accountable, then they could
not possibly consent in any sort of meaningful or binding fashion. It is
interesting that he turns to punishment as a way of demonstrating that
such recognition of accountability is already present in legal practices.
Whether a small village or a state, it is true that some persons are recognized as having greater accountability for their actions, and this is
made most clear through practices of punishment. As Locke points out,
to punish someone for a crime of which she has no understanding or
recollection is nothing but creating misery. The term *punishment*, as
opposed to *cruelty*, implies comprehension that there is logic behind the
pain. For a person to recognize pain as punishment they must have
consciousness. But this is not entirely subjective because society also
recognizes different gradations and elements of consciousness. Hence
punishments are mitigated accordingly.

What Locke presents in *An Essay Concerning Human Understanding* is
a definition of personhood that supports his later elaboration of consent and contractual political order. Yet he turns to extant practices of
punishment as a demonstration of his definition. It seems to me this
provides a corrective to Foucault's work that looks at modern penal
practices as a reflection of Enlightenment notions of responsibility and
individualism. Locke's notion of personhood is elaborated, even sub-
stantiated, in reference to legal practices, not the reverse: the practice
gives rise to the theory.

Another crucial element of the contracting Lockean individual is
established through his discussion of personhood and punishment.
Locke contemplates why society punishes the actions of drunkards, but
not madmen. The common answer is that drunkenness is a state that is
voluntarily entered, while madness descends without volition. Locke
agrees that part of accountability would include being conscious of the
choice to lose consciousness. However, knowing the difference
between the two scenarios—deliberate and involuntary unconscious-
ness—is difficult. "And all that lies upon human justice is, to distinguish carefully between what is real, and what is counterfeit in the
case."[10] Therefore, the social contract is dependent upon this definition
of a person as accountable, yet this principle creates all-new difficulties
for the administration of justice. Locke turns to punishment to establish

an empirical point for his definition of personhood, but practices of punishment render that same person increasingly intangible. The problem that punishment poses for the voluntary, willing individual is especially apparent in the following passage in Locke's *Essay*.

> It is past doubt the same man would at different times make different persons; which we see, is the sense of mankind in the solemnest declaration of their opinions, human laws not punishing the mad man for the sober man's actions, nor the sober man for what the mad man did, —thereby making them two persons: which is somewhat explained by our way of speaking in English when we say an one is 'not himself,' or is 'beside himself.'[11]

Our consciousness may make us a person, but our actions seem to splinter us into two individuals at times. The demands of justice are such that only the fully realized individual may be punished, however.

H. L. A. Hart's *Punishment and Responsibility* is a brilliant rendering of the difficulties of establishing individual accountability when administering punishment. Hart discusses the different mitigating conditions that excuse a criminal infraction as well as determine culpability. Think of all the legal categories that describe differing levels of responsibility for a death: First, Second and Third Degree Murder, Criminal Negligence, Attempted Murder, Manslaughter, Negligent Manslaughter, and Murder in Self-Defense, to name just a few. Hart argues that practices of punishment reveal the difficulty of trying to determine the level of responsibility of a person at the same time that these practices rely upon this idea of responsibility.

Hart proposes that punishment is not actually indicative of individual responsibility—official legal recognition of such intangible aspects of the human psyche such as volition, duress, insanity, compulsion, or self-defense is impossible. The difficulty between determining what is "real" and what is "counterfeit" is too great. Imagine that a man guns down a teenager who had been following him on a dark street for half an hour, convinced that the young man was about to kill him. "I thought he was going to kill me, I thought he had a gun, even though it turned out to be a cell phone." How can we decide if this statement describes self-defense, temporary insanity, murder, or manslaughter?

Instead of actually ascribing clear responsibility, Hart points out that punishment serves to change the relationship of individuals to their world, in making it appear to be more calculable, if not actually become so. Practices of punishment make our environments more predictable by assuming accountability as a norm. We can recall that the first step in Locke's conception of personhood was consciousness defined as the ability to make connections between past and future. The next step he takes is that consciousness then makes people envision themselves in relationship to past, present, and future actions. But another manifestation of this ability to position oneself in a temporal continuum would be the desire and ability to plan and to make choices about present activities with future benefits in mind. Of course things may not always go as planned, and as tempting as it is to see causality in all events (as I explored in chapter 2), sometimes there simply is no link between past and present. Accountability is not ironclad, but assuming accountability is one step toward creating a more calculable world. Hart argues, "If with this in mind we turn back to criminal law and its excusing conditions, we can regard their function as a mechanism for similarly maximizing within the framework of coercive criminal law the efficacy of the individual's informed and considered choice in determining the future and also his power to predict that future."[12]

The relationship between punishment and personhood is ultimately circular. In defining personhood, Locke points to punishment as a reference point. But then practices of punishment bring this definition of personhood into question, precisely by taking Locke's challenge to distinguish between accountable and unaccountable persons. In the end, we cannot rely upon persons having accountability. Someone may have lost his mind that morning, someone may lose consciousness while driving and crash into your car, someone might under orders from a superior flip a switch that releases gas or electric shocks intended to kill. Every day, actions occur for which apparently no person is accountable. But the result of this system is that laws and rights gain accountability, providing a person who may or may not have accountability with an environment with some element of predictability.

Personhood is just one of the pillars of social contract theory; descriptions of the state of nature and natural rights also serve as the foundation for the liberal political order. Locke's account of the natural laws and natural rights that provide the basis for the social contract also rely heavily upon punishment. Locke adopted his ideas of the natural right of punishment from the work of Hugo Grotius, who made the connection between punishment and contract explicitly. In *De Jure Belli ac Pacis* he quoted Michael of Ephesus's *On Aristotle's Nicomachean Ethics,* which observes that in punishment there is "a kind of giving and receiving, which constitutes the essence of contracts."[13] This sounds remarkably like Nietzsche's account of political and social order in book 2 of *On the Genealogy of Morals.* While Nietzsche wants to emphasize the interconnection based upon extraction at the heart of all social orders, I would argue Locke is searching for empirical referents to help sustain his imaginary state of nature.

Locke defines law according to punishment. "For, since it would be utterly in vain to suppose a rule set to the free actions of men, without annexing to it some enforcement of good and evil to determine his will, we must, wherever we suppose a law, suppose also some reward or punishment annexed to that law."[14] *An Essay Concerning Human Understanding* points out three kinds of law: divine, civil, and philosophical law (which he calls opinion or reputation). God punishes or rewards in the afterlife, and upon occasion through divine intervention on earth. Civil law is enforced by magistrates, while social laws, such as etiquette, are enforced through derision and exclusion. Curiously absent from *An Essay Concerning Human Understanding* is natural law, which, as he points out in *The Second Treatise,* implies an ability to punish: "For the Law of Nature would, as all other Laws that concern Men in the World, be in vain, if there were no body that in the State of Nature, has a Power to Execute that Law, and thereby preserve the innocent and restrain offenders."[15] The assertion of natural law was not enough, you needed the evidence that such a thing as natural law did indeed exist. This may be the reason that Locke articulates a natural right to punish: to establish the existence of natural law. After all, even he admits that this position is "a strange doctrine."

Let us consider all of the different useful aspects in his assertion that "every Man hath a Right to punish the Offender, and be Executioner of the Law of Nature."[16] According to his own logic, this demonstrates the existence of natural law, for it would be inconceivable to have law that did not imply punishment. We have the same tautology between accountability and personhood replicated in his idea of natural law and natural right.

The presence of law provokes the necessity to punish. Or is it that the ability to punish marks the presence of law? This is not an idle question. We are more likely to think of punishment following law in order to enforce it. But this leaves unresolved the foundations of political order. Social contract theory delivers the image of men exercising their reason and overcoming chaos to create a more calculable world for themselves. However, all three elements of this scenario—rights, natural law, and personhood—are defined in reference to punishment. Nietzsche's "anti-enlightenment" reading of the social contract is little different from the sources of liberal political philosophers. It may seem that the image of self-regulating rational beings is destroyed by reliance upon punishment to establish the components of the social contract, but for both Grotius and Locke, the ability to punish guaranteed the presence of consent as opposed to coercion.

Grotius presented a more extended consideration of principles and rights of punishment in *De Jure Belli ac Pacis,* but Locke seems to adopt the shorter discussion from *De Jure Praedae Commentarius* almost verbatim. Looking at Grotius's account makes Locke's use of punishment somewhat clearer. The story that most people associate with Locke is present: Grotius accounts for the natural right to punish, quoting from ancient philosophers and the Bible, arguing that the right to punish derives from the right of self-preservation. When we enter a civil society, this right is passed to a political entity. Leaving aside the question of why we would enter such a society for just a moment, consider Grotius's proof for the natural right to punish.

> In the light of the foregoing discussion it is clear that the causes for the infliction of punishment are natural, and derived from that precept which we have called the First Law. Even so, is not the power to punish essentially a power that pertains to the state? Not at all! On the contrary, just as every right of the magistrate comes to him from the state, so has the same right come to the state from private individuals. . . . therefore, since no one is able to transfer a thing that he never possessed, it is evident that the right of chastisement was held by private persons before it was held by the state.[17]

In other words, as all political power derives from individuals consenting to it, the political power to punish must originate in those same individuals. The existence of the political power to punish therefore proves the natural right to punish. This is similar to Locke's assertion that any law needed punishment, and that the existence of natural law proves the natural right to punish. Both arguments are tautological. In grounding civil law in natural law, they turn to punishment as a method of proving the existence of natural law and right, and in asserting its particular relationship to civil society.

Grotius and Locke both invoke the ability of a government to punish aliens as further proof of the natural right to punish. If punishment were purely a political right, then those who had not consented to the government would be unable to be punished. While Grotius seems primarily concerned with using this fact as evidence for natural right, Locke's account betrays an even more pragmatic use of this argument.

> To those who have the Supream Power of making Laws in England, France, or Holland, are to an Indian, but like the rest of the World, Men without Authority; And therefore if by the Law of Nature, every Man hath not a Power to punish Offenses against it, as he soberly judges the Case to require, I see not how the Magistrates of any Community, can punish an Alien of another Country.[18]

In other words, a refusal of the natural right to punish would diminish the authority of colonizing powers—there are pragmatic reasons for embracing the strange doctrine.

The natural right to punish also provides the impetus to join the social contract. As both Grotius and Locke point out, when punishing crimes that have occurred against oneself, we are more prone to anger and lose our natural state of reason. Grotius is particularly interested in pointing out the dangers of exercising our natural right to punish offenders. He spends four pages citing poetry and observations about the weakness of character that emerges in vengefulness. He concludes by offering his most damning account from a poem by Juvenal: "A mind, small, weak, and mean, will ever pleasure take in vengeance. Mark this at once, that in revenge A Woman does rejoice above all others."[19] Nature and reason provide us the ability to punish; the *practice* of punishment, however, can endanger that same reason and nature. One of the primary mechanisms that propel free persons out of their state of nature is the recognition that uninhibited exercise of natural rights creates more discord. Locke argues that in the state of nature, reason reigns supreme. In committing a crime, "the Offender declares himself to live by another Rule, than that of reason and common equity."[20] Others can respond to their infraction and take revenge, but then they too will cease to live by the laws of reason. The same seed spawns crime and vengeance.

The exercise of our natural right to punish endangers our reason. Further, an inability to exercise our natural right to punish endangers our preservation. While Locke emphasizes the danger in exercising this right, think of the frustration and fear that might provoke anxiety in the face of one's natural right to punish. There is a crucial gap between the natural right to punish those who infringe upon your body, rights, or possessions and the ability to do so. Those of poor social stature, no resources, or weak disposition would not have been able to procure justice.

Locke's ideas about punishment make two important additions to Grotius's. Locke defines criminality as irrational, a point that contradicts Hobbes, who at least acknowledges that it can be in one's interest to commit crimes. But in punishing, we do not thereby transfer the offender back into the realm of reason. In his "Second Letter Concerning Toleration," Locke blasts critics of his first letter who argued that religious dissenters should be punished in order to bring them to the correct mode of reasoning. He insists that though crime is a state of war, reason and following the law are not absolutely commensurate. "Will punishment make men know what is reason and sound judgment? If it will not, it is impossible it should make them act according to it. Reason and sound judgment are the elixir itself, the universal remedy; and you may as reasonably punish men to bring them to have the philosopher's stone, as to bring them to act according to reason and sound judgment."[21] Locke points out the futility of using pain to try to inspire reason—that it is far more likely to engender resistance to the power that administers it. Lack of reason will incur punishment, but punishment will not inspire reason.

There is one more aspect of Locke's theory of punishment that has been explored by Nozick that bears mention here.[22] Both Grotius and Locke assert that the natural right to punish demonstrates the natural executive right—it is evidence of our individual power that precedes natural law. While Locke makes the case only obliquely, Grotius is far more forthcoming about the political ramifications of this proof. "Moreover, whatever existed before the establishment of courts, will also exist when the courts have been set aside under any circumstances whatsoever, whether of place or of time. In my opinion, this very argument has served as the basis for the belief that it is right for private persons to slay a tyrant, or in other words, a destroyer of law and the courts."[23] This is a crucial result of the natural right to punish. It means

that anyone who opposes the law deserves punishment, including a
king. If the king uses the law for vengeance, and the interests of the
ruler replace the rule of law, then the people have the right to punish
the tyrant. Grotius argues that anyone who refuses to follow the law
places himself in a state of war with society; the same logic holds
whether it is a murderer or king. The natural right to punish is the
capability that proves the natural executive right. The right of revolution is guaranteed by the natural right to punish, which makes it perhaps the most indispensable element in social contract theory since
consent is immaterial if it may not be withdrawn. Within Lockean theory, punishment becomes a measure of the rule of law, and the final
protection of individual rights.

Punishment and the Perception of a Distinctly Liberal Power

Locke relies heavily upon already existing practices of punishment to
establish the normative principles of his social contract as empirical
precedent. Without punishment, he could not prove the a priori existence of personhood, natural law, or executive powers. He also relies
upon instances of punishment to help distinguish the bounds and
establish the unique character of his political authorities. It is well
known that Locke was uneasy with the creation of the all-powerful
authority in Hobbes. But he does not, as is often assumed by many in
the United States, enthusiastically encourage rebellion against authority. "May the commands then of a prince be opposed? May he be
resisted as often as any one shall find himself aggrieved, and but imagine he has not right done him? This will unhinge and overturn all poli-
ties, and, instead of government and order, leave nothing but anarchy
and confusion."[24]

Locke's attempt to balance the need for order with individual freedom is best surmised through his articulation of tyranny: here he spells
out the privileges and limitations upon liberal power. Like Hobbes's,
Locke's sovereign exists in a special relationship to the law. As in
Hobbes, the sovereign has the power to punish. But here the spirit in
which punishment is delivered becomes, for Locke, the key to perceiving whether the use of executive privilege is within or exceeds the
bounds of acceptable power. In the *Second Treatise*, how a sovereign
punishes is one principal way to judge whether he is a ruler, who
deserves obedience, or a tyrant, who can rightfully be deposed.

In a liberal system, it is understood that the law stands above the ruler; after all, Locke clearly states the difference between a legitimate sovereign and a tyrant: "one makes the laws the bounds of his power, and the good of the public, the end of his government; the other makes all give way to his own will and appetite."[25] The fact that Locke talks about legitimation of sovereignty as its disembodiment reveals his basic understanding of the necessary transcendental qualities of sovereignty. As in *Leviathan,* Lockean sovereignty is based upon transcendental principles, only in this case, it is not semidivine status; instead it is the disembodiment provided by reason that serves as the basis of authority.

This characteristic of Locke's ruler is established through his distinction between the natural right to punish held by all individuals, as opposed to the civil right of punishment awarded to political rulers. In the state of nature, all people have the right to revenge injuries wrought upon them; as a party to the social contract, we relinquish this right. In so doing, Locke points out, we eliminate the state of war from society. Because political rulers are not the victims of crime, they can punish disinterestedly, without cruelty and vengeance. Therefore, the state of war ends with state punishment, rather than being fed as in a cycle of private revenge.

Because this is one of the primary benefits of being in a civil society, a ruler who punishes with revenge in his heart fails to deliver one of the most basic requirements of the social contract. A sovereign who punishes according to emotion, not reason, is by Locke's own definition a tyrant. Therefore, the liberal political order isn't merely dependent upon the exclusive right of punishment and the ability to enforce laws as all regimes are. Instead, the ruler must accomplish order and enforce law, but do so in a very particular manner. This may be the most effective device used to limit state power ever invented: to insist upon reason and calculation even when administering pain to offenders. However, there can be no doubt that this is one of the most difficult principles to maintain in practice, and many commentators have observed that liberal regimes routinely indulge in the pleasures of revenge.[26]

Lest his audience be alarmed that any liberal regimes shall be continually upset by intransigent populations, Locke astutely points out that once the habits of obedience to a ruler are established, they are overturned only with great difficulty. For a ruler to be considered a tyrant, "a long train of Abuses, Prevarications, and Artifices, all tending the same way" must be evident.[27] Locke argues that the substitution of "Will" and "Appetite" for reason and the greater good must be "visible to the People" in order to justify the dissolution of government. This is why in practice, liberal regimes may repeatedly indulge in revenge and cruelty, but leaders not be called to account for the betrayal of principles. The boundaries upon liberal power are entirely dependent upon public perception, not clear regulation. If punishment, no matter how senseless, is perceived as within the boundaries of law, it will be acceptable. Yet because the principle of impartial punishment is elaborated, whenever punishment is perceived as systemically cruel and vindictive, the legitimacy of liberal regimes is called into question.

The fact that Locke uses an explanation of a particular form of punishment to elaborate his vision of sovereign power suggests two different things. First, the disembodiment of the sovereign in the practice of punishment is his way of signaling that this power will be bound, and completely so, by reason. Only the mind will be allowed to rule, and reason is a far less cruel master than the heart. The second element of this description of liberal punishment is more difficult to explain. That Locke is seeking to demonstrate the limited power of the sovereign through the power of punishment is a truly paradoxical task. After all, punishment is a demonstration of power, but in Locke's writing, it is a demonstration of bounded power. The belief that the act of state punishment can demonstrate the limits of state power is a remarkable claim on Locke's part. The fact that the exercise of sovereignty can be taken as an expression of its limits reveals that the "limits" of state power may be far more a matter of perception than empirical measurement. After all, what is considered a pattern of abuses on the part of the sovereign? By what measure can we determine if a ruler is governing with appetite or reason? These judgments are a matter of perception.

Perception, Punishment, and the Social Contract

Jeremy Bentham's work on the social contract proves to be instrumental in helping to understand how perception and punishment serve a uniquely instrumental role in social contract theory. Bentham was made notorious by Foucault's studies of the panopticon, yet it is not his theories of penal practice that interest me here. I believe his ideas about rights and legislation and, even more important, his "Fragment on

Ontology" prove of the greatest interest in relationship to Locke's social contract. Appalled by the overdependence of law and governmental authority upon the fictions of social contract, Bentham offered utilitarianism as a corrective. "The indestructible prerogatives of mankind have no need to be supported upon the sandy foundation of a fiction."[28] Instead, the relationships between state and individual and between private individuals could be grounded in rational and empirical calculation based upon maximization of pleasure and minimization of pain. As Locke adopted the Grotian framework with a new emphasis upon reason, Bentham assumed Locke's interest in reason and abandoned the Grotian framework of natural rights and law altogether.

Though Bentham is often characterized as a coolly calculating utilitarian, he was driven by an adamant desire to reconstruct law and politics upon firm, clearly self-evident grounds. His impulse toward reform was such a primary drive that others observed that "he was the sort of person who could not even play badminton without wanting to stop and design a better shuttlecock."[29] One of Bentham's primary objections to social contract theory and law in general was its foundation upon either a mythical past or an interpreted one. Bentham found reprehensible the practice of viewing the past as the only authoritative source; instead his framework looks to create future good. In *A Fragment on Government*, Bentham fumes against the scaffolding of natural right and original contract that are intended to support sovereignty and obedience to law.

> Conversing with Lawyers, I found them full of the Virtues of their Original Contract, as a recipe of sovereign efficacy for reconciling the accidental necessity of resistance with the general duty of submission. This drug of theirs they administered to me to calm my scruples. But my unpracticed stomach revolted against their opiate. I bid them to open to me that page of history in which the solemnization of this important contract was recorded. They shrunk from this challenge; nor could they, when thus pressed, do otherwise than our author has done, confess the whole to be a fiction.[30]

Ridding himself of fiction, Bentham proposes a different basis for right: punishment. "I say *punished:* for without the notion of punishment (that is of *pain* annexed to an act, and accruing on a certain *account,* and from a certain *source*) no notion can we have of either *right* or *duty*."[31] To understand why this is the case, a cursory examination of Bentham's utilitarianism is needed. He saw maximization of pleasure and avoidance of pain as the clear empirical bases for human action. We may assert rationality as our God, but reason alone cannot overcome these primary impulses. Reason may tell me that I should not take a vacation if I do not have the funds, but it is the threat of creditors that keeps me home. Without any clear consequences for our actions, we would always choose to avoid pain and seek pleasure.

"Nature has placed mankind under the governance of two sovereign masters, pain and pleasure. It is for them alone to point out what we ought to do, as well as to determine what we shall do. On the one hand the standard of right and wrong, on the other the chain of causes and effects, are fastened to their throne."[32] To achieve good behavior, morality needs to be attached to pain and pleasure: we will suffer when we are bad, be rewarded when we are good.

Reason helps us understand the causal relationship between pain and nonperformance of duty. It is up to the state to ensure that punishment is sure to follow infractions, rewards to follow acquiescence. The fundamental shift between Locke and Bentham is that Bentham believes that punishment can influence reason. Not that it creates rationality through pain, only that the assurance of pain administered by the state will change the calculations of every citizen. It may be painful to work, but the pain involved in hanging or incarceration that would result from robbing a bank is far greater than the discomforts of working. In this way, punishment allows the state to manipulate the terms of reason. Any organization of society that attempts to have people do what is right even though they will suffer for it is sure to fail. Reason can be utilized in social order; it cannot serve as the sole basis of it.

This is why though we may be able to understand such a concept as right and duty, this insight will not affect our actions unless we can see a clear manifestation of these abstract concepts in our own lives. Hart and Schofield have commented that Bentham's ontology provides the key to his radical critique of law and politics.[33] Examining his "Fragment on Ontology" reveals that his utilitarianism is actually grounded in the belief that much of reality is founded in perception. He divides the world into categories: those entities that are corporeal and those that are inferential and fictional. Corporeal substances are ones that are tangible such as an animal, mineral, or plant. He has a fascinating test for how one can tell whether the substance in question is corporeal: "Suppose the non-existence of corporeal substances, of any hard corporeal substance that stands opposite to you, make this supposition, and as soon as you have made it, act upon it, pain, the perception of pain, will at once bear witness against you; and that by your punishment, your condign punishment."[34] Take, for example, deciding that the cars driving by in the highway do not exist. You step into the traffic, only to have the existence of the cars affirmed when you find yourself in an ambulance on the way to the hospital.

The situation with inferential substances is quite different. "Suppose the non-existence of any inferential incorporeal substance, of any of them, and the supposition made, act upon it accordingly,—be the supposition conformable or not conformable to the truth of the case, at any rate no such immediate counter-evidence, no such immediate punishment will follow."[35] I could wake up and bleakly assert that love does not exist. Whether or not there is love in my life, there is no immediate counter to my sad assertion. Someone could do something that demonstrated love to me that day which might make me change my mind, but love itself, free of all agents, could not demonstrate that my bleak denunciation was wrong.

It is tempting to conclude that punishment serves as the basis for empiricism, but this would be incorrect. Instead, punishment serves to create the perception of reality, or not. Love may exist, but it needs an agent to make it appear, while the cars need no such messenger. These passages assert a kinship with Hobbes's theories of nonrepresentational perception and his theory of sovereignty. Therefore, while Bentham's critique of social contract theory as a fiction seems particularly damning, it becomes clear that all abstract categories such as sovereignty, rights, and law would fall into the same category.

> Necessity, impossibility, certainty, uncertainty, probability, improbability, actuality, potentiality;—whatsoever there is of reality correspondent to any of these names, is nothing more or less than a disposition, a persuasion of the mind, on the part of him by whom these words are employed, in relation to the state of things, or the event or events to which these qualities are ascribed.[36]

The problem of politics then, is how to make these abstract entities appear to be real, to have people perceive them as real. Punishment is the way that abstractions such as morals, rights, duties, and sovereignty gain an empirical existence. The enforcement of laws and duties through punishments is what makes us perceive them as real. Contract, as another noncorporeal entity, cannot serve as the translation of rights and duties. This would be, in Bentham's terms, using fiction to prove another fiction. Bentham insists that rights and duties only become real when they cause pain or reward.

The fact that Locke's formulation of law, rights, personhood, and contract keeps returning to the practices and notions of punishment to serve as an empirical referent suggests that perhaps the essential views of Locke and Bentham are not as far apart as they initially appear. Take away Locke's story of the contract, and all you have left is punishment to serve as the foundation. However, to say that right and personhood is based in punishment requires unflinching pragmatism.

Bentham's ontological theory also suggests why political institutions play such a central role in the formation of consciousness and perception of the world. He argues that the state is the "strongest and surest" mechanism in its operation—the entity that will most reliably administer punishments and rewards to meet our perceptions and actions based upon those perceptions. Other entities, such as schools, friends, and parents, can also provide punishments and rewards, but they do not have the "sufficient force" to give these other suppositions "any practical value."[37] Therefore, the power of the state to punish in a way that no other entity in our world can, by administering death or incarceration, is what gives the noncorporeal entities it enforces a stronger existence than most inferred substances—friendship, love, community, to name a few. While we may experience these entities, and they may give us pleasure, they are not enforced with the same vigor as the law. Hence, according to Bentham it would be impossible to arrange a society based upon the sure cause-and-effect relationship between the rewards or loss of friendship. The power of the state to punish, along with the will to do so vigorously, literally structures our reality; it makes political principles more central than all others.

This assertion immediately provokes the question of what happens when the state fails or refuses to punish offenders. Does this mean that we lose the most central points of orientation in our grasp of abstract reality? Do other principles arise and become more central than the law and sovereignty? Do we struggle to maintain a sense of right and duty, ultimately failing in our ability to believe these fictions "that deal in sounds instead of sense"?[38] If we are to take Bentham's assertion seriously, then punishment would be the primary duty of a state: in punishing it creates the reality of sovereignty, it makes the laws empirical, and it orders the conceptual universe of its citizens. This is an unyieldingly difficult view of the possibilities of human organization and justice, which is why the metaphor of contract is more generally acceptable, even if they amount to the same thing.

Liberal State Power and U.S. Penal Practices

Therefore, we can see that social contract theory is dependent upon practices of punishment in an entirely unique sense. Because liberalism is based upon abstractions such as the social contract, natural rights, and even personhood that have no empirical referent, it has from the very start relied upon practices of punishment to make these terms operable. If practices of punishment are needed for theoretical explanation, making the power of the liberal state evident is certainly more difficult. Yet this is a difficult matter, for if just making state power evident were enough, liberalism would be no different from other forms of government. However, punishment in liberal regimes is intended to make government evident, but as a limited, not absolute power. Punishment establishes the two core elements of a liberal regime: its emphasis upon the rights of individuals and the bounds upon state power.

Critical reflection on contemporary U.S. penal practices reveals that they do shadow the arguments I have outlined in this chapter. First of all, the government has largely relinquished the aim of producing or changing reason through punishment; therefore there is currently no justification for penal practices based upon reformation. The U.S. government recognizes the rights of prisoners without seeking to bolster the capacities that presumably create those rights. The ambiguous tautology between practices of punishment, rights, and personhood present in the foundational texts of liberalism continues today. The state punishes to emphasize personal responsibility but through punishment often denies that same sense of self and culpability. We do not punish to bolster individual rights and personhood as much as to assert that these things exist already.

Some people argue that corrections has become a gruesome industrial complex, an economic engine in its own right. While certainly some people materially benefit from incarceration, I believe these industries grew because the opportunity was there, and now these organizations and towns defend their territory, unnaturally prolonging the impulse toward severity. However, private corrections firms and rural local governments cannot be understood as the root cause of mass incarceration today. Instead, we can see how current incarceration creates, as Hart observed in 1968, the expectation of accountability and personhood, rather than the actual product. I will explore this theme in relation to neoliberal economic policies in the following chapter. Choice, labor, and citizenship are reinforced as basic freedoms in an era of deindustrialization through the deployment of mandatory labor in penal institutions.

While the terms of liberalism are clearly at play in contemporary penal practices, the struggle over the limits and scope of state power is also evident. David Garland has made a powerful argument that the new severity in the United States and Britain is a reflection of changing definitions of state power. Both regimes have aggressively rolled back the entitlements of citizenship in the past thirty years. This decline in welfare and other social entitlements reflects a larger shift in the relationship between the state and its citizens. Political freedom has been redefined to highlight individual freedom, exercised through the market and the capacity for personal choice, instead of an emphasis upon political freedom that is guaranteed by social and economic stability. The decline of the welfare state and the growth in incarceration both emphasize individual choice and the private freedoms of the market. But they are complementary in another sense: the economic disparities resulting from neoliberalism produce more fiscal insecurity and instability. Polarization of income levels creates fear of crime, while the loss of the safety net combined with deindustrialization creates more economic anxiety. Both of these fears can be visibly, and dramatically, met by the state as it steps up to vigorously control crime. People feel more secure in an unequal world when the government adopts more rigorous policing methods. The state may be providing a different kind of security than it used to, but has proven its continued indispensability.[39]

While I agree with Garland's argument, I continue to be mystified why such vigorous policing and the incarceration of so many citizens has been considered acceptable in a historical era marked by distrust of government and a desire to have less regulation. Crime is certainly one of the great exceptions to this overall social trend in both the United

States and Great Britain. Though Garland persuasively shows us how punishment and social control meet the new insecurities caused by a reduction in state entitlements, how can a social movement so greatly at odds with the prevailing philosophy of government flourish? What can account for the exceptional status that is awarded to state power in the area of punishment in liberal regimes?

Part of the answer to this question is provided by Locke. In his theory, liberal state punishment actually represents bounded and limited state power: punishment is a method of representing the limitations of the state rather than its coercive capacities. In many ways this is entirely counter to any logic—after all, the state is exercising domination over bodies in a fashion that is considered completely unacceptable under any other circumstance. The fact that these activities are perceived as an expression of measured authority can help account for the lack of alarm on the part of the general public.

Whether or not the governments of Britain and the United States are pursuing rational and just penal practices, the populations of these two countries perceive them to be acceptable. Thus it becomes more important to understand why particular groups support punitive punishment and why others do not see it as an issue that is central to larger questions of justice and right in their own lives. Marie Gottschalk has recently completed a study of interest group politics and institutional trajectories that explains the unexpected sources of support for new severity in the United States. Reaching back into the 1920s, Gottschalk examines the deep institutional roots that help provide legitimacy for punitiveness. More recently, she looks at identity interest groups and also advocates of prisoners' rights from the 1970s that unwittingly contributed to the mass incarceration of the 1990s into the twenty-first century.[40] Clearly the racialized nature of mass incarceration plays a central role in the lack of identification with those languishing in prisons in the United States.

However, religious tensions and different ethnic identification did not prevent average Americans from feeling absolute horror at the abuse of prisoners in Abu Ghraib. Though Garland and Gottschalk help to explain the lack of popular outcry over the incarceral explosion of the last twenty years, we cannot assume that public apathy will continue in the future. When a train of abuses becomes "visible," and when the standard of reason is applied, rather than assumed, with respect to methods of punishment, there may yet be a day of reckoning and reform. Locke established the highest standards for the norms of liberal governance; however, enforcement of these standards falls to the perseverance of the people. The real question is whether the habits of obedience will continue to trump the intangible ideals at play, and whether these ideals can truly be wielded to redistribute power.

CHAPTER 6

Hitched to the Post

Prison Labor, Choice, and Citizenship

> The gods had condemned Sisyphus to ceaselessly rolling a rock to the top
> of a mountain, whence the stone would fall back of its own weight. They
> had thought with some reason that there is no more dreadful punishment
> than futile and hopeless labor.
>
> —Albert Camus, "The Myth of Sisyphus"

Systems of punishment and economics have been mutually constitutive throughout history. Colonization and penality proved to be convenient partners for hundreds of years. It is relatively easy to understand convicts as a source of exploitable labor and hence discern a causal relationship between capitalist development and punishment in the modern era. Certainly, accumulation of wealth has driven methods of punishment repeatedly. The exceptional cases interest me, however—what can we say about prison labor in an era of unemployment? What is the logic behind prison labor if expropriation of wealth is not the primary goal? Does prison labor cease to support capitalism, or has the relationship between the two become more complex? This chapter argues the latter point, that today prison labor and ideas about punishment reveal shifts from late industrial to postindustrial economies. I also explore the ideological function prison labor serves within contemporary U.S. capitalism. By focusing on how punishment shifts along with the economic system, it becomes clear that punishment serves a crucial function in political economy in general; exploitation of labor is only one manifestation of this relationship. In the context of the United States, citizenship is one of the primary mechanisms by which punishment comes to enforce political economy.

Labor and Citizenship

The problem of how to make people embrace wage labor has been with us since industrialization. In order to produce surplus value, work must be separated from mere survival and valorized on its own terms. John Locke made an early attempt to specify how labor serves as the foundation of citizenship within the social contract in *The Second Treatise of Government*. Here he specified, "Labor put a distinction between them and common"—the act of labor takes nature's bounty, which is shared by all, and turns it into individual property. Because every man "has a property in his own person"—his labor—every man who labors is thereby eligible, and motivated, to participate in the social contract that establishes a government.[1]

In a recent article, Nancy Hirschmann explored Locke's "Essay on the Poor Law" to see how his theories were developed in relation to the laboring classes of his time. He advocated cutting public relief to paupers, since it was through work that people developed reason and the capacity for liberal citizenship. Failure to work or poverty "was evidence of a failure to *use* their God-given rationality."[2] Thus, at the time Locke was developing his theory of the social contract he perceived that linking citizenship to labor was one way to ensure the stability of liberal forms of government. The mythical founding of the social contract on labor solves several problems. First, labor becomes a proof of a person's willingness to exercise rationality as well as self-discipline, both characteristics that are sorely needed in a liberal polity. Second, according to Locke's schema, labor creates property, which provides the impetus to consent to and uphold the social contract. This answers the question why we would ever choose to trade natural freedoms for political ones. Finally, whether intentional or not, the connection between work and citizenship also served to support industrialization in England.

In Locke's version of citizenship based upon labor, there is one exception to his rule, slaves.

But there is another sort of servants, which by a peculiar name we call slaves, who being captives taken in a just war, are by the right of nature subjected to the absolute dominion and arbitrary power of their masters. These men having, as I say, forfeited their lives, and with it their liberties, and lost their estates; and being the state of slavery, not capable of any property, cannot in that state be considered as any part of civil society; the chief end whereof is the preservation of property.[3]

Here, Locke provides the philosophical basis that later helped to justify the exclusion of slaves from citizenship in the United States. Labor is the crucial step in making one fit to join the social contract—it establishes your *individual* stake in and claim upon the world that was previously held in common. Because as a slave you do not even own your own labor and cannot create property, you become ineligible for citizenship. Interestingly, Locke also explains that indigenous populations do not mix their labor with the soil in the same way as Europeans and therefore do not create private property for themselves either. Locke's social contract prefigured the racially exclusive form of American citizenship through his linkage of work, reason, and the mythological foundation of the social contract.

In her book *American Citizenship* Judith Shklar makes a convincing argument that Locke's valorization of labor was central to the founding of the United States.[4] She points out that the work ethic was a conscious fashioning of American identity in contrast to the aristocracy of the Old World and the chattel slavery of the New World. Aristocrats were maligned for their parasitic existence, and slavery was detested as the specter of unprofitable and underpaid work. Between these two poles, a life of leisure and the horror of enslavement, Americans glorified the reward, dignity, and character-building effects of labor.

While there are no formal work requirements in the Constitution, the United States has linked the rights of citizens to wage labor in social policy. As Alice Kessler-Harris has recently explained, "Unlike many other industrialized countries, America chose to distribute what the British social theorist T. H. Marshall called the rights of 'social citizenship' on the basis of work rather than as a function of residence or citizenship."[5] The U.S. government has developed a host of benefits that accompany wage work, including social security and unemployment insurance. Health care is linked to wage employment rather than citizenship as well. According to Kessler-Harris, wage work has also served to differentiate levels of citizenship, particularly starting in the twentieth century with New Deal programs.

Work, wage work, had long marked a distinction among kinds of citizens: intimately tied to identity, it anchored nineteenth-century
claims to political participation. But when the federal government
linked wage work to tangible, publicly provided rewards (i.e., social
security and unemployment) employment emerged as a boundary
line demarcating different kinds of citizenship.[6]

Kessler-Harris explores how women and other minorities have been
and continue to be systematically denied "social citizenship" based
upon their failure to participate in the formal wage market. Although
originally, as Shklar points out, the ideal was to work for oneself and
gain true independence, today wage labor is considered the opposite of
an unhealthy "dependence." Debates about welfare suggest that participation in the formal workforce is still considered a mark of character in the United States.[7]

Though the principle linking labor and citizenship may be traced to
Locke, his original formulation is not feasible in the United States
today. Shklar's and Kessler-Harris's works suggest that the connection
between citizenship and work changes over time. Today, in practice,
we have linked labor and citizenship not through the notion of property but rather *choice*. When one chooses to work, labor is a sign of
maturity and a capacity to self-govern. In contrast, when one is forced
to labor, labor becomes a punishment and actually makes one less fit
for citizenship. Hence, examining forced labor practices in the United
States allows us to consider which populations are made unfit for citizenship as well as to investigate how the relationship between work
and citizenship is currently defined. Furthermore, it is crucial to
remember that forced labor is a form of *labor* and as such reveals contemporary economic trends.

During eras of expanding economies and full employment, the ideological connection between work, choice, and citizenship seems perfectly reasonable. But what about times of economic stress? If it
becomes clear that not everyone can choose to work, then a society
needs to recognize and accommodate this fact. During the Great
Depression, the U.S. federal government expanded social welfare programs in order to provide political stability by meeting the needs of its
citizens. These welfare programs assumed that citizens had rights independent of their status as workers and that the government owed a
basic level of support to citizens. The adoption of welfare reversed

Locke's assumption that citizens, as workers, will provide a basic level of support for government.

However, we live during an era when neoliberal theories have enjoyed renewed prominence, as evidenced in multiple arenas: the reduction of corporate regulation, reduction of tariffs, elimination or severe restriction of social programs, downsized taxation, and privatization. These transformations have reinforced, if not accelerated, the traditional American valorization of work and the understanding that employment serves as the gateway to full citizenship. This ideological connection of work, choice, and citizenship has become ever more insistent at a time of structural unemployment. How do we reconcile the opposing theory and reality?

This chapter argues that the tensions between neoliberal ideologies of work and contemporary realities of unemployment are clearly ascertained through the lens of prison labor. I also argue that prison labor itself has become a spectacular means by which this tension is "resolved." However, as I shall explain, the ideologies of free choice and work have become increasingly difficult to maintain, which has led to ever more farcical performances of penal labor.

Social theorists have frequently observed that the penal system is developed in conjunction with the needs and detritus of the economic order. Jonathan Simon, Malcolm Feeley, and David Garland have pointed out that the penal system in the United States has experienced a shift in orientation. While one aspect of the penal system is to provide a clear moral order for a society, Simon and Feeley argue that this "New Penology" notably lacks a coherent narrative or purpose. "It has not yet succeeded in producing a viable truth about crime."[8] The result is increased anxiety about crime and a lack of confidence in the institutions that deal with it. Garland, on the other hand, argues that the welfare state created a form of penal welfarism. Both regimes "meshed effectively with the new mechanisms of social regulation, with government through experts, and with ideological stress upon universal citizenship and social integration that characterized social politics in the post-war period."[9] It was the decline of universal citizenship and post-war prosperity that undermined the welfare state and, alongside it, penal welfarism. Garland observes a "sharp discontinuity" in penal practices that reflects the turn toward neoliberalism in both in the United States and Great Britain.

Garland offers his observations as a contrast to Simon and Feeley's.

The sudden shift in penal policies *does* make sense given the larger historical, economic context. However, both analyses can be correct. Penal policies are not coherent narratives, but that is because they reflect current ideologies and economic developments. Contemporary prison labor is an expression of deindustrialization in the United States and the loss of employment in urban and rural areas. I am not arguing that prison labor is *caused* by these shifts. Rather, this particular incarnation of forced labor practices in the United States reflects and *hides* these political, economic trends. It deliberately contests economic reality outside prison walls, and this is why it becomes incoherent and unable to produce "a viable truth about crime," as Simon and Feeley observe.

Forced Labor in Historical Perspective

In order to understand what distinguishes forced labor practices today, it is illuminating to consider how they differ from other episodes of involuntary labor in U.S. history. Because of the radically disproportionate number of minority, male inmates, prison labor today is frequently viewed as a return to slavery. This impression is reinforced by the fact that prison labor is made legal through a clause in the Thirteenth Amendment. Slavery and involuntary servitude are outlawed in the United States, "except as punishment of crime whereof the party shall have been duly convicted" (U.S. Const. Am. 13, Sec. 1). Certainly, the legality of forced labor in penal institutions has rested upon this "escape clause" in the Thirteenth Amendment. In 1871, the Supreme Court of Virginia, in *Ruffin v. The Commonwealth,* determined that a convicted felon "is for the time being a slave, in a condition of penal servitude to the state," hence "civically dead," lacking rights normally awarded to citizens.[10] Joan Dayan has also pointed out in her work that the practice of chaining inmates together to work, tracking inmates with bloodhounds, and monitoring working inmates with armed guards vividly evokes the history of slavery in the United States. The visual references to the era of slavery are particularly disturbing when considering the racially disproportionate prison population.[11] Furthermore, the practice of many states denying convicted felons the right to vote in perpetuity does suggest the creation of a permanent caste of noncitizens and a new era of Jim Crow in the twenty-first century.[12]

Despite the ghastly family resemblance between slavery, disproportionate minority confinement, and forced labor practices today, there are crucial differences. The *Ruffin* ruling no longer stands, and prisoners' rights are recognized (if not always maintained). More important for the purposes of this argument, slavery was an integral part of the early national economy. Low-cost labor was essential for the agriculturally dismal territory of the South. Slavery made it possible to turn a profit from a swamp. While it was without a doubt fueled by racial animus and aristocratic fantasies, slavery was an institution that served an economic purpose. Prison labor today is abysmally unproductive, a fact I shall explore later. Incarceration is not driven by the need to extract low-wage labor from inmates.

Similarly, many people would consider the convict lease system in the postbellum South an extension of slavery. However, in his study of the convict lease system, Alex Lichtenstein argues that despite appearances, the convict lease system was not a functional equivalent to slavery. On the contrary, Lichtenstein found that convict labor was used in new industrial sectors of the economy, enabling the South's rapid industrialization following the Civil War. Rather than accept being burdened with the costs of a free labor force, nascent industrialists developed infrastructure with the use of extremely cheap labor. Convicts built the roads and railroads, stoked the furnaces, and removed the coal that marked the death of the plantation economy. Agricultural exploitation remained in force through the sharecropping system, but convict labor forged the new economy that proved to be even more profitable in the long run.[13]

Immediately after emancipation, industrialists were faced with a recalcitrant labor force. Newly freed slaves were not eager to sign up for lengthy workweeks, even for wages.[14] Industrialists complained that even working freed slaves chose to work only two or three days a week, preferring free time to more wages. The convict lease system solved the dilemma perfectly: industrialists were given a new captive labor force. Furthermore, Lichtenstein argues, the convict lease system provided a method of discipline for poor black families in rural areas as well. Not fulfilling sharecropping obligations led to threats of the chain gangs. "Since it reinforced, rather than disrupted, the form of social control necessary for extreme labor exploitation in the South's plantation districts, this was a form of 'modernization' acceptable to planter and industrialist alike."[15]

What is important to note here is that the convict lease system provided labor discipline for those outside the purview of the chain gang as well. This fact was not lost upon workers in the industries that used convict labor. One committee issued a report to the governor of Georgia urging him to restrict the use of the convict lease system. They argued prison labor was

> offensive to the just pride of that worthy and estimable portion of our community [the white working men]. They feel that the natural effect is to degrade their vocation, by turning out from the walls of the Penitentiary the worst characters as rivals and associates in their business.[16]

While the concern for competition from convicts whose wages were minimal is evident, workers also adopted elements of the rhetorical and ideological stance that had helped to defeat slavery: Republican free labor.

Eric Foner's book *Free Soil, Free Labor, Free Men: The Ideology of the Republican Party* explores how the ideology of free labor was used to challenge slavery. Rather than contest slavery on purely moral grounds like the abolitionists, Republicans made the argument that it was important to banish slavery from the Union because it sullied the heart and soul of the United States: free labor. In speaking of differences between the Southern and Northern sides of the Mason-Dixon Line, Thomas Ewing observed, "Labor is held honorable by all on one side of the line because it is the vocation of freemen—degrading in the eyes of some on the other side because it is the task of slaves."[17] Alexis de Tocqueville shared this concern in *Democracy in America,* making the argument that slavery was debilitating for the slave but also for the master, killing his capacity for innovation and desire to work. Clearly, forced labor was viewed in relation to free labor: its presence in the United States had consequences for all.

Reviewing this brief history of the convict lease system presents an interesting point of comparison to the economic circumstances of today's prison labor. Lichtenstein points out that the convict lease system was an integral element in the South's rapid industrialization in providing inexpensive, unskilled labor. Today, by contrast, the United States is suffering from deindustrialization. The only sector of the unskilled labor market that is experiencing growth is the service sector. For the most part, prison laborers are entirely unsuited to fill this niche. Telemarketing jobs are one large exception, but the vast majority of service sector jobs could not practically or cost-effectively be fulfilled with prison labor. Therefore, unlike the convict lease system, contemporary prison labor serves no pressing need on the part of the market.

Furthermore, convict lease labor was extremely productive. Today, UNICOR, the Federal Bureau of Prison's work program, loses money every year. In response to labor activism in the 1930s, Congress passed the Ashworth-Summers Acts that made it a felony to transport or sell prison-made products across state lines. In 1979 the Federal Prison Industries Enhancement Act (PIE) was passed allowing private companies to enter into joint ventures with prisons. In order to be exempt from the Ashworth-Summers Act, prison workers must be paid the federal minimum wage. (It is important to note that 80 percent of wages paid to prisoners are passed on to prisons for their overhead expenses or to the justice system to meet the costs associated with conviction.) Joint ventures in prisons are now in place in thirty-six states, and 80,000 workers are engaged in commercial activity behind bars. Examples of prison industries include hotel reservations, office furniture, blue jeans, lingerie, and electrical wire.[18] The largest employer is the Federal Prison Industries UNICOR program, which employs 21,000 workers, primarily making goods for the government under mandatory sourcing contracts.[19]

UNICOR does not have to pay prisoners a minimum wage as it is already in compliance with the Ashworth-Summers Act because it sells to the government. Even with wages as low as 21 cents an hour, UNICOR products are expensive, costing on average 13 percent more than the same goods provided by private firms.[20] These products are shoddy; one study found that wire supplied by UNICOR failed at twice the rate of other suppliers. Finally, UNICOR delivered its products late 42 percent of the time.[21] Clearly, UNICOR would not be able to compete in an open market. It seems that having a captive buyer and next-to-free labor would be tremendously profitable. Why isn't prison labor more lucrative?

The difficulties with doing business in prisons are numerous. Security costs are high, much higher than the wages of the workers. For example, in 2001 in the Philadelphia Prison System 350 inmates (out of the 22,124 prisoners who were taken in) were released for work assignments. In the same year, the prison conducted 2,494 security checks on these 350 inmates![22] Machinery installed in prisons does not tend to be the most efficient or up-to-date, and productivity is interrupted by lockdowns or security disturbances at the prison. There are difficulties in conducting manufacturing in prisons ill-designed for the purpose. For example, trucks delivering supplies could not fit between two security gates encircling the prison that were programmed to open only one at a time. Inmates are released from the prison, creating high turnover rates and a need for constant training, particularly since those employed in prison industries are most likely low-risk, nonviolent offenders. It is true that employee absenteeism is low, and companies do not have to pay payroll taxes, unemployment benefits, sick leave, or retirement, nor enforce worker safety or environmental requirements. Ultimately, the balance sheet seems to come up even: employers would be just as well-off looking for nonincarcerated workers.

This is not to say that there have not been attempts to make prison labor more market savvy. Two institutions in Texas have taken the lead in trying to reform the current prison labor system, the Enterprise Prison Institute and the Criminal Justice Center at the National Center for Policy Analysis. Morgan Reynolds and Knut Rostad have testified before congressional hearings and produced studies arguing that prison labor might be used with greater profit in the United States. Both men testified at a hearing for HR 4100 entitled "Free Market Prison Industries Reform Act of 1998," which proposed ending mandatory sourcing regulations, lifting interstate restrictions on products made in prisons, and privatizing Federal Prison Industries, making it possible to sell products on the open market.

Proposals to privatize and expand prison labor profited from the labor shortage of the late 1990s. A brief entitled "Creating Factories behind Bars" points to the "93% unemployment rate behind the gates of American prisons" as a solution to "a workforce shortage that threatens American competitiveness."[23] The benefit of prison labor extends beyond private manufacturers to taxpayers and prisoners as well. They argue that 80 percent of income earned by prisoners currently is returned to the criminal justice system or helps pay compensation to victims. Expanding prison labor would be one way to manage the costs of the policy of mass incarceration. Finally, prisoners who work in prisons are 24 percent less likely to return to prison after release. While Reynolds and Rostad imply that this is due to the training and discipline provided by work experience, this may also be attributed to the fact that only the best behaved prisoners are allowed to work.

Reynolds and Rostad cite gross public mismanagement for the underutilization of the workforce behind bars in the United States.

> However, since prison industry is usually state run rather than privately run, the output is often shoddy, overpriced merchandise that other state agencies must buy from the prison industry monopoly. The largest prison supplier was the Federal Bureau of Prisons with $433 million in output for federal agencies, yet the system employed only 16,000 inmates out of 61,000 inmates eligible to work (i.e., those not in solitary confinement, considered dangerous, or being transferred) from its total of 85,000 inmates.[24]

Today, the number of inmates has risen dramatically, but UNICOR still employs only a fraction of potential workers. The globalization of manufacturing has played a key role in hearings about prison labor; as Senator Mitch McConnell asked, "How about the apparel makers who use offshore labor? A lot of apparel is produced overseas now. Do you think we could find a way to entice them back, with some of them using prison labor?"[25] Despite some support, the proposed reforms have not thus far been approved.

The failure to push prison labor into the free market does not seem to be due to a reluctance to privatize government functions on the part of the current administration. Nor can the strength of unions take credit in this regard. I believe prison labor is unattractive to most investors because they do not need the kind of labor that prisoners can supply. McConnell may have fantasies about recapturing a manufacturing sector in the U.S. economy through the competitive deployment of prison labor, but even at slave wages, American workers cannot compete in the global marketplace anymore. And this may be the primary reason that so many potential workers are behind bars in the first place.

Troy Duster argues that the "darkening" of U.S. prisons can be directly linked to deindustrialization in American cities. In 1933 black people were incarcerated at approximately three times the rate of white Americans; in 1990, the rate was eight times that of white persons.[26] This shift in the pattern of incarceration can be compared to the loss of jobs in manufacturing in large cities and the concurrent rise of service sector employment. Because service sector jobs rely much more on fronting the image of the company, minority youths are far less likely

to be able to land these jobs that now dominate the entry level employment market. For instance, racial differences in language patterns are
particularly sharp in the United States. Duster cites an experiment conducted by William Labov, a linguist at the University of Pennsylvania.
Labov tape-recorded the voices of children at playgrounds in London
and in Philadelphia. Neither he nor his English colleagues were unable
to identify the race of the children recorded in London. In Philadelphia,
however, they could four times out of five. Because service sector jobs
hire on the basis of employee presentation and the image of the store,
Duster argues that significant differences in language have meant that
African American youths have been displaced out of the labor market
in the transition to a service sector economy.[27]

Continuing to look at Philadelphia as an example, the city has suffered from high structural unemployment, has abysmal public schools
that are primarily attended by African Americans and other minorities,
and has surprisingly low property values. Philadelphia also has an
incarceration rate that is 148 percent of the national average and a significantly younger (35 percent of inmates are 24 or under) and dispro-
portionately African American (72 percent) inmate population. Sixty-
eight percent of inmates in the Philadelphia prison system are there for
dealing drugs or theft of some kind.[28]

Two sociologists, Bruce Western and Katherine Beckett, have argued
that the extraordinary incarceration rate in the United States in the
1980s and 1990s has seriously distorted typical measurements of unemployment. Taking the tremendous incarcerated population into
account (2 million people according to the *New York Times* on May 19,
2003) raises the overall unemployment rate for men by 1 percentage
point. This would make the current unemployment rate closer to 7 percent. However, because of disproportionate minority confinement, taking incarcerated populations into account creates a 5-percentage-point
rise in African-American male unemployment. Including frustrated job
seekers and prisoners into their calculations, Western and Beckett place
African American male unemployment at 38 percent, even during the
"recovery" of the 1990s! Western and Beckett argue that penal institutions need to be understood as a labor market institution with two general effects: first, to hide massive structural unemployment; second, to
create decreased job performance on the job market for those exiting
them.[29]

A point of historical contrast makes this second effect all the more salient. In his book on the parole system, *Poor Discipline*, Jonathon Simon points out that during the era of indeterminate sentencing in 1960, in order to be released on parole, prisoners in thirty states had to show that they had been offered gainful employment.[30] Such job offers did not always materialize, nor was the system any guarantee that ex-offenders seamlessly melded back into society. But such a provision is unthinkable today, not only as a condition of release, but also in comparison to the employment restrictions that are placed upon ex-offenders upon their release. Both federal and state governments bar ex-offenders from holding jobs that require federal or state licenses. These occupations include working airport security, as aids in nursing homes, or as a social worker. Those with drug convictions cannot obtain student loans.

Prisons work more to remove large numbers of the unemployed from public view and to further stigmatize them. Especially in perpetuating the population's unemployment status after release, prisons play in a key role in the hardening of poverty in U.S. cities. Simon argues that work provides the main method of achieving "normalization" in American society, and so unemployed persons on parole are not likely to be reintegrated into communities. He argues that given the structural unemployment in cities, to break the cycle of incarceration we will have to develop "an understanding of the normal distinct from the discipline of the labor market."[31] While I absolutely agree with him, I believe that contemporary prison labor practices suggest exactly why this is not likely to be the case. After all, if prisons are helping to mask what are extraordinarily bad economic prospects for minority youths in the country, then why have them labor in prison at all?

The Moral Economy of Work or Work as Punishment?

Two different traditions intersect in prison labor. One is the tradition of work as rehabilitation; the other is work as punishment or discipline. The residue of both traditions can be found in debates about prison labor today. The tradition of work as penance and rehabilitation has been with the institution of the prison since its inception. In Eastern State Penitentiary in Philadelphia, Tocqueville and Beaumont described prisoners who were kept in their cells in solitary confinement for the entire length of their sentence, in order to prevent criminals from further contaminating one another. The original penal institution, the Walnut Street Jail, discovered that individuals kept in solitary confinement without activities went insane. At Eastern State Penitentiary, the Quakers improved upon the model of solitary confinement by adding handicraft activities for each prisoner to accomplish in his cell.

> It is highly remarkable, that these men, the greater part of whom have been led to crime by indolence and idleness, should be constrained by the torments of solitude, to find in labor their only comfort. By detesting idleness, they accustom themselves to hate the primary cause of their misfortune; and labor, by comforting them, makes them love the only means, which again free, will enable them to gain honestly their livelihood.[32]

Work becomes the welcome respite from idleness, and prisoners view work as a form of redemption, a proclivity that reformers hoped would continue after release as well. The Auburn penitentiary model also placed a great deal of emphasis upon the rehabilitative aspects of labor in prisons. By having prisoners work collectively but in absolute silence, they learned the self-discipline and obedience needed for collective production. Interestingly, as Thomas Dumm points out, the system of rehabilitation through work was developed in the United States during a time of an acute labor shortage, so released prisoners were likely to be able to ply their trade after release.[33] According to Tocqueville's interviews, the work of prisoners was also used to defray the costs of confinement, an advantage that is also frequently mentioned today.

Today some prison reformers advocate increasing work release programs, allowing prisoners to gain work experience, earn some money, and enjoy more humane conditions of confinement through a variation of their everyday activities. As I already mentioned, one rationale for expanding prison labor is decreased recidivism. Most prisoners today would prefer to work. Days are monotonous, and even dreary tasks are more welcome than solitary confinement. Supermax prisons that place prisoners in cells for twenty-three hours a day are finding that solitary confinement causes insanity just as it did two hundred years ago. Dealing with overcrowded prisons, wardens and guards welcome prison work. It provides occupation for the prisoners and wears them out, making them a more tractable population. Within the institution, prison work provides the sole occupation for prisoners now that educational and recreational budgets have been slashed.[34]

But I believe that prison labor serves a different function outside the prison walls. David Goldberg has observed that the labor discipline provided for minority men in prisons and the workfare assignments created largely for minority women outside of prison enforce capitalist moral economy. "In the moral economy, then, prisons are supposed ideologically to represent law and order, work in the face of welfare, discipline rather than delinquency, social control over anarchy."[35] Foucault also observed the intricate way that the penitentiary is closely calibrated to the economy outside of it.

> How is power to be strengthened in such a way that, far from impeding progress, far from weighing upon it with its rules and regulations, it actually facilitates such progress? What intensificator of power will be able at the same time to be a multiplicator of production?[36]

Viewed in this light, prison labor takes on a special significance considering that it is becoming more popular just at the time that structural unemployment in urban areas has emerged as a permanent reality. Today prison labor affirms that our old assumptions are still valid: those who do not labor are criminals. What more efficient way to insist upon participation in the workforce, even at a time when such participation becomes more difficult?

Examining the debate over the State of Oregon's Measure 17, which was passed in 1994 requiring all prisoners to work forty hours a week, we can see the interlacing of different, often contradictory arguments about the nature of work, choice, and citizenship. Because the debate happened during a period of economic prosperity, a common argument was that requiring prisoners to work was a form of rehabilitation and would reduce recidivism. Interestingly, there was also resentment on the part of taxpayers that they were paying for prisoners to remain idle while *they themselves* were required to work forty hours a week or more.[37] Prefiguring the Personal Responsibility and Work Opportunity Act of 1996, the popularity of Measure 17 in Oregon (it passed with 71 percent of the vote) suggests that voters will not endorse exemption from work. The ideological linkage between work and moral character that I began this essay by describing still remains very strong.

The problem with this logic is that the incarcerated population comes from the population least likely to find work in the first place, and it is even more disadvantaged on the job market after serving time in prison. The ideology of work and citizenship in the United States dictates that all rational and disciplined people can and will choose to work. Not being able to work is a reality that our understanding of citizenship, virtue, choice, and freedom simply cannot accommodate, particularly in an era of increased market discipline. To acknowledge that some people cannot work would require a fundamental shift away from neoliberalism. Yet such a dramatic shift seems unlikely, even in the face of growing structural unemployment. The incarceration boom hides some unemployment, and prison labor maintains the fiction that unemployment is a character, not an economic, issue. This is the logic by which we pursue prison labor practices of another era, sometimes with absurd results. It is this collision of ideology and a changing economic reality that has led to some of the incoherence that Simon has noted in contemporary penal practices.

Prison Labor as Farce

In *State of North Carolina v. Clifton Frazier* (COA00–122, 6 February 2001), the State Supreme Court ruled that Clifton Frazier could not be convicted of larceny for stealing from the prison canteen where he was assigned to work. Frazier was paid one dollar a day for his labor. Over the course of three months, $665.75 worth of goods and money disappeared from the canteen. The initial conviction found Frazier guilty of larceny, but the Supreme Court overturned this conviction, arguing that he was not an employee, by definition. "Defendant did not make a wage that would have been lawful outside of prison, he could not lawfully refuse a work assignment, and he had no bargaining power or any of the other ingredients of a traditional employment relationship." Some prisoners are paid the minimum wage but still by law are not employees. The key distinctions here seem to be the ability to choose whether or not to work, and the sense that work is a reciprocal relationship between worker and employer.

But establishing these two precepts as the basis of free labor may be problematic, and become even more so. If one cannot find a job, is employment still a choice in any regard? If there is a shortage of jobs, do employees still enjoy a reciprocal relationship with their employers? Economic anxieties are making these questions more pressing. The case of *Larry Hope v. Pelzer* illuminates how the connection between work and choice is maintained, even in absurd circumstances.

In Alabama, prisoners who disrupt work on the chain gangs or who refuse to work on the chain gang are disciplined by being chained to a hitching post, outside, with their arms high above them. There are regulations of this practice: prisoners are to be offered bathroom breaks and water, and prisoners are to be released once they state that they are ready and willing to work in the chain gang. In 1994, the Department of Justice conducted a study of the Alabama Department of Corrections' use of the hitching post and found that these regulations were only sporadically followed. The DOJ advised Alabama to desist in its disciplinary use of the hitching post—particularly because, they argued, not all prisoners were released when they said they would return to work. In short, it was acceptable for the hitching post to be used to enforce participation in prison labor, other than that it was considered inappropriate. Remarkably, the Alabama Department of Corrections replied that they would continue to use the hitching post "to preserve prison security and discipline" (*Hope v. Pelzer*).

A case decided by the Supreme Court in summer 2002 provides a vivid picture of the use of the hitching post in Alabama. Larry Hope, a prisoner, was affixed to the hitching post twice. The first time was due to a disturbance between himself and two other inmates on the chain gang working together. He was removed and attached to the metal apparatus for two hours. The incident was well documented in the prison records, including the times that he was offered bathroom breaks and given water. When he agreed to resume his work, he was released from the hitching post and returned to the chain gang. The second time Hope was punished with the hitching post followed an altercation with the guards of the chain gang. His shirt was removed, and he was held in the hot June sun without water or bathroom breaks for seven hours. Guards offered him water, then poured it on the ground in front of him, taunting him about his thirst. Hope brought a civil case against the guards who were ruled to be immune from prosecution. The Supreme Court overturned this decision, ruling that reasonable persons should have known that such activities constituted cruel and unusual punishment, and that the guards were thereby liable for their actions.

The scene is striking, a man, attached to a metal bar, hands in shackles above him. He is dehumanized thoroughly, and in order to regain his "freedom," he must emphatically state that he will choose to go work on the chain gang. Why go to such perverse lengths to make the prisoner "choose" work? On one hand, the insistence that the prisoner choose reaffirms the ideological connection between labor and citizenship. Prisoners will be punished until they are willing to use their reason, their "free will," as society would dictate. On the other hand, to enact choice in such a fashion is actually quite dangerous. It is just as easy to say that such an exercise reveals Hope's "choice" as entirely fabricated. Perhaps, after all, work is not really a choice.

Prison labor becomes a painful enactment of social normalcy in one other way as well. Now that tougher economic times have hit the state, Oregon voters do not like the idea that convicts are able to secure employment when those on the outside are finding it increasingly difficult.[38] Voters overwhelmingly amended Measure 17 in 1998, restricting the use of prison labor, and even further restrictions were demanded by the AFL-CIO and ultimately delivered by the state in 2002. There is little talk anymore about the rehabilitative purpose of prison labor. We want prisoners to labor, but we don't want them to compete. Hence, we have the development of spectacularly unproductive labor.

In Alabama and Arizona, for example, wardens have decided to pay for large boulders to be brought to prisons. Convicts break these boulders into gravel with hammers. The gravel, of no practical use, is deposited into pits next to the prison.[39] The prison pays to bring in more boulders to be smashed. This is not work as rehabilitation or training, this is not work that is generating profit. This is work as punishment. In Oregon, where the most public debate about the relationship between free and forced labor has occurred, some have even suggested that convicts should be employed in pushing boulders back and forth over highways. The ultimate punishment devised by the gods for the man, Sisyphus, who dared to scorn their rules migrates out of the underworld onto the earth's surface.

But Camus reminds us that the primary distinction between Sisyphus and other workers is the hero's consciousness of the futility of his labor. In chapter 2, I looked at what this passage says about consciousness and the limits of human rationality. Here I want to highlight the element of labor in the myth.

If this myth is tragic, that is because its hero is conscious. Where would his torture be, indeed, if at every step the hope of succeeding upheld him? The workman of today works every day in his life at the same tasks, and this fate is no less absurd. But it is tragic only at the rare moments when it becomes conscious.[40]

To say that prison labor, particularly in this guise, is absurd is not to dismiss the pain, both physical and mental, that such labor inflicts upon those forced to engage in it. Unlike Camus, I cannot imagine prisoners smashing boulders as happy. But in the sense that recognition of the absurd provides for an elevated level of consciousness, I present these final manifestations of prison labor as the absurd in precisely that spirit. The myopic view that all rational people will choose to labor at a time when structural unemployment is becoming a permanent reality is creating the need for farce. An insistence that participation in the labor force is always a matter of rational choice, not social opportunity, becomes increasingly difficult to maintain.

The U.S. political and economic systems have been sustained by the ideology linking citizenship and labor. But maintaining this construction is requiring that a significant proportion of our population, particularly black men, be sacrificed. The unemployed are branded as criminals, removed from public view, and permanently crippled in their attempts to participate in the workforce. Releasing prisoners from the burden of maintaining this fiction for the rest of us should be enough provocation to dismantle the links between choice, labor, and citizenship. In case it is not, we would do well to remember the origins of the treadmill. Tocqueville points out that treadmills, "machines that work without producing," were developed in English prisons in 1822 to provide constant activity for prisoners without undue competition for other workers.[41] At the time, it was inconceivable that such a machine would find its way out of the prison. How curious, almost two hundred years later, it has become a common metaphor for understanding the experience of work and leisure, the rhythms of modern life, even outside the walls of the prison. Endorsing rock crushing, boulder pushing, or any other form of labor, purely for the sake of laboring, shows how far we have traveled from Locke's initial calculation that labor is fundamentally a matter of rationality.

CHAPTER 7

Punishment and the Spiral of Disorder

We have previously shown, and histories everywhere teach, that wars are usually begun for the purpose of exacting punishment.
> —Hugo Grotius, *De Jure Belli ac Pacis*

The season is changing.
Return me my freedom!
Oppressive government and cruel treatment—
One day there will be revenge.
> —Poem written on a wall of Angel Island Internment Center

The focus of this book has been punishment and the birth, development, or reconsolidation of political orders. Correct deployment of punishment helps to establish the guiding principles of a regime and establish legitimacy for an authority in a given populace. It can also help shape the political economy of a regime, playing an integral role in the material support of political order. But I would not want to perpetuate the idea that punishment only serves to bolster the power of the state. Too frequently punishment has been understood as the expression of inviolable power, and naturally, this perception serves the power of the state, as I argued in my discussion of sovereignty. Therefore, I want to conclude with a case study of how punishment can also be a catalyst in the unraveling of regimes, and how it can at times demonstrate the state's powerlessness.

Like all the other dynamics this book describes, the role that punishment plays in the creation of political disorder cannot be pinned down. Definitive statements such as "whenever practices of punishment contradict a regime's political ideals, political instability occurs" are impossible. After all, at times practices of punishment do contradict a regime's stated ideals, and it causes no interest, critique, or disruption whatsoever. Nor does the severity of punishment seem to play any decisive role in whether a regime is stable, so it cannot be argued that

147

the specific form of punishment particularly matters. Instead, the *perception* of unjust punishment as emblematic of political power creates instability. It is impossible to explain public perception in its totality, but it is the key to the other elements of this argument. What transforms punishment into an injustice is perception. Once an instance of punishment is perceived as an expression of the state's power, rather than the criminality of the person being punished, a fundamental shift has occurred. Punishment has ceased being an unquestioned and given activity and become an opportunity to judge the state's exercise of its given authority.

In conclusion to this book, I am going to discuss recent practices of punishment by the United States in Iraq and Guantánamo Bay. As established in chapter 5, domestic penal practices are leniently viewed as an exception to limited state power, and even the incarceration explosion has not served the same generally catalyzing role as events in these prisons located abroad. U.S. penal practices have come to be emblematic of the U.S. government in the international arena in a dynamic remarkably similar to the horror recounted by the travelers in More and Kafka. The reverberations are also felt at home of course, but the horror over Abu Ghraib largely results from the fact that U.S. citizens know that people all around the world are scrutinizing these actions so closely. Nothing brings on self-examination like the view of an outsider.

Transcripts of prisoners in Abu Ghraib and Guantánamo Bay demonstrate that they experience their abuse as a form of punishment. Indeed, it is clear that Americans are asserting a command and control over others through confinement. If the ability to punish could be simply equated to the power of command, then the extreme actions taken in these confinement facilities would mark an ascendance in American power. But this is not at all the case. In fact, I argue the exact reverse; these instances of power reveal ill-conceived attempts to reassert American control and reassert a clear causality within an ever deeper spiral of disorder. The more vigorously American soldiers, commanders, agents, and guards try to construct a logic of America supremacy in their prisoners and in the international arena as a whole through punishment, the more powerless the country becomes.

Toward a Paradigm of Punishment and Political Disorder

Practices of punishment, and people's responses to them, are an indicator of the authority and legitimacy, hence stability, of a regime. Punishment reveals people's perceptions about their political order and at times can galvanize sentiment in opposition to that regime. This is because punishment offers a clear vision of how ideas of justice and the exercise of power intermingle: punishment offers an opportunity for everyone to see to what end a regime exercises its power. At times, practices of punishment, as in the theories of Locke, reveal a ruler to be a tyrant—it is no accident that the Soviet gulags, Saddam Hussein's torture chambers, and Chinese prisons are often cited as evidence of the corrupt nature of these regimes. When punishment belies ideals, practices of punishment can undermine the stated principles of the state and result in political disorder. Admittedly, this is not always the case. Sometimes practices of punishment betray, for example, the doctrine of equality, and yet the inequality reflected in practices of punishment raises nary an eyebrow.

Therefore we cannot say that punishment simply demonstrates whether a state has the power of command. Nor can we say that the way a state punishes will determine whether it is perceived as legitimate. We need a more complex analytical paradigm that takes into account three different dynamics in the relationship between authority and punishment. First, authority and legitimacy are the result of a relationship rather than a unidirectional expression of force. As I established in my discussion of sovereignty, political power is contingent upon relationships between the authorities and those subject to it.

Second, we also need to take into account the theatrical elements in this relationship. Political authority needs to be presented as such and cultivated as such; this is an insight central to political philosophy. This is a more complex matter than first appears because any authority that must pointedly assert itself is already weakened. Therefore the presence of authority needs to be perceptible, but without an overinsistence upon itself. For example, if a parent needs to point out that he has authority over his child, he has already lost his authority even though stating his authority may appear to be an assertion of an existing hierarchy.

In the case of punishment, it may be tempting to use penal systems to assert control that is lacking in other arenas. This logic is inherent in all state punishment since crime is a lapse of legality, therefore punishment is a reassertion of the rule of law. Protesters who refuse the legitimacy of the government in general or some of its specific actions will be met with punishment that reasserts the exclusive power of the law. As we saw during the civil rights movement, if policemen assert the power of the state and go beyond the rule of law, for example, by beating generally peaceful protesters, punishment can actually catalyze opinion against the state in favor of the protesters. Punishment as an expression of authority can be counterproductive in given contexts.

This instance is related to my final point. In the case of state punishment, authorities need to demonstrate that they deserve their unique privileges because they serve the larger interests of justice (or at least have a presentation that they serve justice that convinces most people). As soon as punishment is entirely about the power of command it becomes counterproductive. Punishing to demonstrate a disparity of power will quickly destroy the tenuous connection between power and justice cultivated by all regimes.

Hannah Arendt's essay "On Violence" can provide some assistance in elaborating this model. In this essay, Arendt complicates the common assumption that the state's capacity for violence serves as the source of its authority. Like sovereignty, authority is relational and can be undermined by those subject to it. Interestingly, Arendt argues that the real source of authority comes from those subject to it, not those holding it. If those subject to an authority cease to view it as such, authority withers. She distinguishes between power and authority by arguing that power comes only from the ability of people to act together. It is the power of the people to grant authority to the state; the state can never command authority through the gun, whip, or jail.

"Power and violence are opposites, where one rules absolutely, the other is absent."[1] In situations of extreme violence there is no ability to act together to assert collective power, and order is disrupted. Violence may generate obedience, but according to Arendt, it cannot create power. A battalion running through a village shooting guns may separate the inhabitants and send them running—but not until the battalion comes together and starts to organize itself can we say that power has changed hands. When the people rule absolutely there is little opportunity for violence. This is the principle behind town watch organizations and mass demonstrations. "The extreme form of power is the rule of all against one, the extreme form of violence is one against all."

Two valuable aspects of Arendt's essay are her insights about the relational aspects of authority and the self-defeating impulse to use violence to maintain power. First, a person who has the power of command can lose it if her relationship with her audience changes. Authority's "hallmark is unquestioning recognition by those who are asked to obey; neither coercion nor persuasion is needed."[2] If you have to explain why, for example, the state is allowed to punish criminals while angry mobs are not, the state does not have exclusive political authority. "To remain in authority requires respect for the person or the office. The greatest enemy of authority, therefore, is contempt, and the surest way to undermine it is laughter."[3] If a policeman hands you a speeding ticket and you laugh and rip it up, or if a person on trial giggles during sentencing, authority is put into question.

How authorities react in such a situation is revealing. If the policeman then handcuffs and kicks the driver, his own authority becomes further undermined. "To substitute violence for power can bring victory, but the price is very high; for it is not only paid by the vanquished, it is also paid by the victor in terms of his own power."[4] Every instance of criminality provokes this dilemma. An infraction of the law is a provocation to political authority. The punishment will work to reinforce that authority or it could undermine it. In some instances it is conceivable that the state, feeling absolute certainty of its authority, would barely respond to those that challenge it. As Nietzsche observed, "As the power and self-confidence of a community increase, the penal law always becomes more moderate . . . it is not unthinkable that a society might attain such a consciousness of power that it could allow itself the noblest luxury possible to it—letting those who harm it go unpunished."[5] Imagine a social structure so strong that there was no need to punish to prove might, right, or law. The giant has no need to swat at the gnat. On the other hand, a state could respond vehemently, insisting upon order for even the slightest infraction. The now popular "broken windows theory" comes to mind here: if you let small things slide, then the larger ones are sure to follow. If you draw a line in the sand refusing to tolerate *any* asocial behavior, then accordance with the larger issues will come even more naturally. Such vehement policing demonstrates political power remarkably unsure of itself.

But these are the extreme examples, and most of the likely instances of punishment fall between these two poles of vigilance and laxity. Arendt also equivocates from her original position: though power and violence are distinct they "usually appear together."[6] Punishment is a combination of authority and violence; the state's authority, bestowed by others, allows its representatives to inflict pain and to commit acts of violence *that are not perceived as such.*

One can think of instances of punishment as a sort of Rorschach test—incidents that reveal different people's relationship to a given political authority. Punishment is seen as violence if the state is not recognized as legitimate. For example, take Emma Goldman's critique of prisons and call for their abolition.[7] Because in her eyes the state has no legitimacy as an institution of justice, Goldman looks upon confinement as a form of kidnapping, and a constraint of human bodies that goes against natural rights. On the other hand, those who see the state as legitimate beyond question will never perceive punishment as a form of violence.[8] In both of these scenarios, the given view of the state determines how the punishment is perceived; it does not depend upon the particular practices of punishment.

A third possibility most accurately captures the dynamics of state punishment and the generation of authority, however: instances of punishment can either build up the legitimacy of a regime or undermine it in the eyes of those who are not strongly inclined toward either of these ideological poles. An insecure authority who punishes to demonstrate the power of command seeks to reassure her sense of authority and demonstrate to the world that she has power. Punishment most evidently intended as a demonstration of command will most likely fail to generate authority. So while punishment can reveal a perception of a regime, it can also change one's perception of that regime. If a practice of punishing appears to be too strident, questions emerge as to whether the state uses its entrusted powers wisely. If a state goes out of its way to be particularly humane in practices of punishment, as practiced in Philadelphia in the years immediately following the American Revolution, legitimacy may be accrued.

The necessary element of pain in punishment makes it a dangerous exercise for the state. As political authority has become ever more abstract, decentralized, and bureaucratic, thus lessening any potential resistance to the exercise of political power, state punishment becomes more and more of an anomaly. Because punishment serves to lessen the authority of the person doing it, the distinction between the sovereign and the person who acts in the name of the sovereign becomes crucial. The agency behind punishment today is occluded since there is a representative of the state, rather than the state itself, inflicting pain. Nonetheless, punishment does assert a relationship between the state and the body of a citizen; furthermore, it is the one instance where the state deliberately inflicts pain upon someone subject to it. All of the disciplinary mechanisms in the world do not change these basic realities of state punishment. For this reason, the authority of the state is most at risk when it exercises the prerogative to punish.

Because punishment generates resistance, we would assume that those who have been punished would have a less than favorable view of the state. Beyond that, systemic instability comes when even those who witness practices of punishment become disturbed by the manifestation of power. Once this happens, the legitimacy of the political order is at stake. A dramatic example of this dynamic is provided by the public response to incidents of prisoner abuse in occupied Iraq and Guantánamo Bay. Here the assertion of U.S. power in the punishment of prisoners and detainees has led to an unraveling of U.S. political power in the world. It currently appears that the effects of prisoner abuse shall remain limited to the international arena and have not led to a delegitimation of the regime domestically, though the scandals caused a significant drop in support for the war in Iraq among civilians in the United States.

Punishment at Abu Ghraib

> They took me to the room and they signaled me to get on to the floor. And one of the police he put a part of his stick that he always carries inside my ass and I felt it going inside me about two centimeters approximately. And I started screaming, and he pulled it out and he washed it with water inside the room. And the two American girls that were there when they were beating me, they were hitting me with a ball made of sponge on my dick. And when I was tied up in my room, one of the girls, with blonde hair, she is white, she was playing with my dick. I saw inside this facility a lot of punishment just like what they did to me and more. (Sworn statement provided by Detainee #151365)

The seemingly ever-widening prison abuse scandal in Iraq, Afghanistan, and Guantánamo Bay reveals the importance of perception in maintaining political authority and the danger that punishment can pose to the legitimacy of political power. When Secretary of Defense Donald Rumsfeld traveled to Abu Ghraib only days after the scandal broke in May 2004 he referred to the pictures and reports of sadism and torture and declared, "This does not represent us." The problem for Rumsfeld and the United States is that, very quickly, the

images of prisoner abuse did come to represent America in the minds
of many Muslims in the Middle East and around the world. For those
who found the power and intentions of the United States already suspect, the photos proved beyond any doubt that the United States is
morally corrupt and sexually uncontrolled, and uses power for self-
gratification rather than justice. It would have been impossible to imagine a more effective propaganda campaign for recruitment to the resistance. Even two years after the original scandal of prisoner abuse had
been made public, in February 2006 Australian news services created
another round of outrage around the world and discomfort for the U.S.
government when it broadcast additional images from 2003 that had
not before been made public.

The prison abuse scandal at Abu Ghraib broke just as I was complet-
ing the plans for this book. I vacillated whether a discussion of the
events was appropriate in the context of punishment. After all, it was
never called "punishment" in our newspapers, but rather "torture" or
"interrogation techniques." The United States had captured people, but
they had not been sentenced. The United States confined people to fight
terrorism, not to punish terrorists. But in most of the sworn affidavits of
prisoners from Abu Ghraib that were reproduced in a collection of documents pertaining to the abuse, Karen Greenberg and Joshua Dratel's
The Torture Papers: The Road to Abu Ghraib, prisoners described the
actions taken against them as "punishment." While the terminological
difference may be due to the translators, it becomes clear from studying
the stories of the prisoners why the framework of punishment fits the
patterns of abuse in Iraq and Cuba.

When reading the affidavits of prisoners who were abused in Abu
Ghraib, they refer to different episodes during their confinement as
"punishment." This is remarkably different from the public discussion
of these events in the United States. Those particularly outraged by the
abusive practices have labeled them "torture," hoping to shame the
U.S. government into reform. Administration officials refer to the practices as "interrogation techniques." These two labels are not as different
as they sound since both imply a motive in administering pain outside
the logic of reciprocity inherent in punishment. Torture is employed
when a state wants to break down resistance, neutralize political opposition, generate obedience, and demonstrate its power in the clearest
possible fashion. The state asserts complete control over the body of the
subject in custody, demonstrating that the exercise of its political power

is unbounded by anything—including the rule of law or any conception of human, political, or natural rights.

"Interrogation techniques" implies a state of war or emergency
when the rule of law is formally suspended—either in a general or
highly specific manner—in order to perpetuate sovereignty. In a state
of emergency, a state may suspend the normal procedures of law under
the assumption that this suspension is necessary to protect the regime.
This follows the logic of "sovereign exceptionalism" as described by
Schmitt and, more recently, Agamben. In a state of war, the state and
the military may violate the rights of others who are suspected of
endangering the lives and rights of other citizens because they are considered enemies of the state and therefore enjoy none of the usual political rights. The administration has justified abuse of detainees in Iraq,
Afghanistan, and Guantánamo Bay with this rationale. Under pressure
from Congress to consider closing Guantánamo facilities in June 2005,
Vice President Dick Cheney said that the remaining detainees were
"bad people" and also that an untold number of terrorist attacks have
been prevented through the detentions and interrogations. However,
he also defended interrogation practices at the facility in terms of executive power, claiming that any attempt to regulate treatment of prisoners would be a "restriction" on executive power, making it more difficult to fight the War on Terror.

To see the prisoner abuse as torture or interrogation techniques is
actually less disconcerting than to think of it as punishment, precisely
because wartime strategies and torture are understood to be outside of
the normal political order. Looking at these episodes as punishment
assumes that these policies and actions reflect our political order, our
method of rule, and our commitment to the rule of law. Referring to an
action as punishment implies that it is a more or less sanctioned activity to establish a relationship between a regime and those subject to its
punishments. When a state punishes, it does so intending to correct
behavior on the part of the person deemed an offender, to send a message to other potential offenders and deter future crimes, or in retribution for the pain caused by the offender. Even though it is done through
extralegal channels, what has happened in Abu Ghraib, Guantánamo
Bay, Afghanistan, Camp Nama, and most likely other detention facilities that we do not know about reveals a combination of all three of
these impulses.[9] Looking at these activities as punishment helps to
establish the pattern and logic, and ultimate danger, of the violence.

One of the more interesting aspects about contemporary prisoner abuse by the United States is how it has come to be managed in relationship to the law. The U.S. administration has done everything in its power to define these activities as extralegal. Doing so will allow the state to plead for the clemency afforded by exceptionalism, and it also helps to make the case for the necessity of these actions. The central claim is that our current political situation is so dangerous that extralegal actions are necessary; however, the relationship can be reversed as well: the fact that we are doing extralegal actions must mean that our current political situation is exceptionally dangerous. Through the establishment of these extralegal channels, the administration simultaneously achieves a carte blanche to punish without any boundaries and can claim that these practices do not reflect our interpretation of the law, rights, or justice.

Though we have seen the suspension of the rule of law and the right of habeas corpus before in the United States with President Lincoln's startling assertions of executive war privilege, there are some new elements in this episode. The government has created a special area, Guantánamo Bay, where the United States can exercise sovereignty extraterritorially. The United States can do things to prisoners in these spaces that it would not be able to do on American soil. The government is separating the exercise of sovereignty from its boundaries of the nation-state, and whether this shall be a precedent or an exceptional circumstance remains to be seen. Since the Geneva Convention applies to prisoners of war, and fundamental political rights apply to prisoners within the United States, it would appear that international and domestic law would provide all the necessary protections to individuals. However, the special category "enemy combatant" allows for prison abuse to happen outside of normal legal channels. Through these administrative categories the state can engage in the abuse of prisoners without being in direct conflict with the law.

The legal maneuvers that make it possible to explain in complex detail why no laws have been broken, and why exactly these practices stand outside the United States' human rights record, may be technically correct. U.S. courts may continue to grant exceptional status to these practices, ironically enough, providing legal protection for these extralegal activities. But it is clear that world opinion does not accept that these images and activities are somehow exceptional and necessary. Instead, the detention facilities have come to represent the U.S.

government around the world. Furthermore, it is widely assumed that the abuses have official government sanction and reflect clear intention. In other words, unlawful detainment and prisoner abuse is regarded as state punishment by the world audience, and any state that punishes in such a manner is clearly unjust.

The prison abuse scandal and penal practices have damaged the reputation of the United States and limited its ability to serve as a check on other regimes' abuses. In March 2006, China took the unprecedented step of producing a rebuttal to Washington's annual report on human rights abuses that labeled China as one of the world's most systematic offenders against human rights. In its press release, China urged the United States to spend its energies examining its own problems, including the enormous incarcerated population, discrimination against minorities in the judicial process, and police and prison abuse. The report also mentioned the abuse of human rights by the U.S. government, "both in and outside the U.S.," referring to prisons and confinement centers in Iraq, Afghanistan, and Cuba.[10]

In Iraq, a public opinion survey completed in May 2004, just weeks after the photos of detainee abuse in Abu Ghraib were publicized, demonstrates that the scandal caused a rapid deterioration in the perceived legitimacy of American forces in Iraq. Sixty-one percent of those interviewed assumed no one would be punished for the abuse at all. Fifty-four percent of respondents assumed that "all Americans" behaved like the guards in Abu Ghraib who were responsible for the humiliation and deaths of detainees.

Soldiers too were profoundly affected by the scandal. It is important for military morale for soldiers to feel that their mission is just, that their sacrifices and privations are for a greater cause. As soon as the photos became widely circulated, surveys of the troops found that morale had dropped significantly. Soldiers in Iraq quickly recognized that these images of abuse would define the occupation in minds around the world. They fretted that all of the good work that had been done in Iraq was forgotten at the very least and completely undermined in some regard. How could they be confident that they stood for human rights, justice, moderation, and peace? The public's perception was also dramatically changed by the images of prisoner abuse. In a CNN/USA Today poll taken the week after the scandal broke, for the first time a majority of Americans expressed discomfort with our role in Iraq, and the majority felt that our mission was compromised.

World opinion sees the abuse of detainees as sanctioned by the U.S. government and hence perceives this as state punishment. Examining the transcripts of testimony taken from prisoners in Abu Ghraib and Guantánamo Bay, it becomes evident that there is good reason for the prisoners to experience abuse as pursuing both retributive and reformist logic. The prisoners who provided statements about their experiences in Abu Ghraib present them in terms of punishment. When Charles Graner beats, starves, and handcuffs one detainee, he responds by saying, "Then I told him I did not do anything to get punished this way so when I said that he hit me hard on my chest and he cuffed me to the window of the room about 5 hours and did not give me any food that day and I stayed without food for 24 hours."[11] Another detainee recounts a series of incidents with his guards as a series of invented punishments. "The first punishment was bringing me to Room #1, where they cuffed me high for 7 or 8 hours . . . And one day in November, they started different type of punishment, where as American Police came into my room and put the bag over my head."[12] They experience the treatment as having a rationale, a cause and effect. At times, even the Americans collecting the affidavits from prisoners and MPs in Abu Ghraib fall into the same terminology, for example asking about activities during "punishment time."

The detainees assume that their treatment is punishment that is administered for a reason. They were on the losing side of the war, the Americans do not like their religion, and their pain is a clear demonstration of the fact that they are now subject to American authority. Remarkably, virtually none of the affidavits mention that the MPs are asking them questions or trying to obtain information from them. Though the appeal for special powers rests upon the need to extract information, the abuse of prisoners does not seem to be consistently related to gathering information.

One striking element of the texts describing the abuse of prisoners at Abu Ghraib is the hostility toward the Islamic religion. Looking at the actions outside of their dubious relationship to the law, you can begin to see an unacknowledged logic at work. Their actions make it clear that religion is perceived as the barrier between these detainees and their acceptance of the power of the United States. In a memo concerning one prisoner in Abu Ghraib, the commanding officer Pappas provides the following assessment.

Detainee is at the point where he is resigned to the hope that Allah will see him through this episode in his life, therefore he sees no need to speak to interrogators. Detainee will not answer open-ended questions, has a smug attitude and is running counter approaches on interrogators. Detainee needs to be put in a position where he will feel that the only option to get out of jail is to speak with interrogators.[13]

Their treatment is meant to be rehabilitative, getting them to renounce their religion, to see that their God has failed them, and to change their perception of how the universe is ordered from a religious model to a secularized one. Over and over, guards worked to fundamentally restructure the belief systems of their detainees and have them accept American power as more fundamental than their religious belief. The Qur'an is sullied, specific rituals are denied, and regulations are broken including contact with women, forced grooming, and public nakedness.[14] The punishments seem calculated to replace a belief in transcendental authority with an acceptance of worldly power. Punishment is the restructuring of perception, the inscription of cause and effect, and the demonstration of sovereignty. However, it is apparent that trying to force a conversion from the worldview of Job to that of Hobbes is counterproductive to say the least.

In another regard, the abuse can be seen as an attempt, not to produce reformation, but rather as deterrence. Terrorist attacks made the United States look and feel vulnerable. In order to prevent future terrorist attacks, it needs to demonstrate its might. Stated differently, the detentions and abuse may be a declaration of U.S. sovereignty in a Schmittian sense: the government suspends the law, not because it needs to, but to demonstrate that the U.S. government can, and will.[15] The extraterritorial jurisdictions in Guantánamo Bay and the abuse in Afghanistan and Iraq might not only be about avoiding legal restrictions, but it may also be construed as a demonstration of the geographical expanse of American sovereignty.

The UN report on Guantánamo Bay observed that the U.S. military serves as "defense, judge, and executioner" in the cases of the detainees.[16] The bizarre structure of legal proceedings, largely engineered with the help of the U.S. court system in response to challenges such as *Hamdi v. Rumsfeld,* almost seems determined to produce just

this impression of totalistic power. The policy on detentions and toler-
ance of prisoner abuse may not actually be aimed at extracting information, especially since torture produces only the most suspect knowledge in any circumstances, but rather the logic of deterrence. The
images of abuse in Abu Ghraib and stories from Guantánamo Bay are
contemporary equivalents of heads placed on spikes next to the fortress
walls, all done in the name of a Leviathan unrestricted by territory.

Or this may be simply retribution. The prisoners assume that they
are being punished in retaliation, and in some indirect sense, they are
correct. The abuses in Abu Ghraib must be viewed in relation to the
inability of occupying forces to exert control over the rest of the country. Several transcripts recounted that specific instances of abuse were
presented as retaliation for roadside bombings and insurgent attacks
on U.S. armed forces in Iraq. In February 2006, a Guantánamo Bay
detainee stated in an interview with the BBC: "If anything bad happens
to the United States anywhere in the world, they immediately react to
us and treat us badly, like animals. It's understandable they would
treat us that way."[17] Lack of control outside these facilities leads the
United States to exact revenge upon those vulnerable to its control. This
impulse to revenge is palpable in Iraq, which is why the continued perception on the part of the American public that there was a direct connection between the terrorist attacks in New York and Washington and
the invasion of Iraq is not as misguided as it initially appears.

The Abu Ghraib case demonstrates many of the elements of my theoretical discussion about sovereignty, perception, the rule of law, and
the exercise of political power. The primary way that the state can punish and cause pain without appearing to be violent is to do so within
the bounds of law. They will punish no more nor less than the letter of
the law: in this way the state demonstrates it is rationally prescribed
how they go about punishing, rather than being motivated by fear or
anger. The spirit of punishment is presumably legal, not personal, and
therefore the pain and violence is fundamentally different than the pain
and violence inflicted by one individual or group of individuals upon
others.

When punishment appears to go outside the bounds of law, a state
can save face by proclaiming that the law was broken, and that those
who broke the law will be punished. In doing this, they will stand for
the rule of law, even persecuting those among their own ranks who fail.
This is reminiscent of Machiavelli's counsel when it comes to using
strict discipline to supplicate a given population. It may upon occasion

be necessary to use cruelty to supplicate an intransigent population. But Machiavelli wisely counsels that then the instrument of cruelty needs to be sacrificed. Cesare Borghia provides this example in *The Prince*.

> And as he knew that the harshness of the past had engendered some amount of hatred, in order to purge the minds of the people and to win them over completely, he resolved to show that if any cruelty had taken place it was not by his orders, but through the harsh discipline of his minister. And having found the opportunity he had him cut in half and placed one morning in the public square at Cesena with a piece of wood and blood-stained knife by his side.[18]

In contrast, President Bush announced on May 20, 2005, that full justice had been done to the few miscreants in the service of the U.S. military, the day after yet another damaging report of prison abuse in Afghanistan had been leaked. "Regardless of rank, every person has been held accountable," he claimed. This assertion is belied by the fact that the commanding officer in charge of military interrogations at Abu Ghraib was issued a written reprimand.[19] Others have noted that the Bush administration has actually rewarded those responsible for promoting the policies leading to the abuse. Some congressional representatives understand the symbolic importance of the handling of the prison abuse scandal. On June 22, several Republican and Democratic senators called for a congressional inquiry into prison abuse, stating, "we need to prove that we are a rule of law nation."[20]

Though reform seems slow in coming, as the administration insists that these quasi-legal practices are necessary, nonetheless there is a new concern to at least appear as though the United States respects the rule of law in other regards. Since the prison abuse scandal broke, there has been more attention paid to whether soldiers are fighting according to the rules of engagement. "By any means necessary" is no longer acceptable, at least in front of the American public. There are points where the strength of the actions themselves can break through the interpretive model that is provided to situate them. The deployment of prisoner abuse photos and stories has accomplished this task. It has changed the frame of reference by which we understand the U.S. role in Iraq.

The need to assert our authority in relationship to the law is driven by the context of the Iraq war. The United States invaded Iraq without the blessing of the United Nations. This invasion was largely predicated upon the failure of Hussein's regime to follow the rule of law; hence he was considered a danger to the world at large. Like the emergency suspension, our invasion was justified on the grounds that it would ultimately create a more stable international regime. In these circumstances it is particularly important to prove that our actions do fall within the bounds of international law.

In other circumstances, when the legitimacy and authority of a government's regime are not in question, there is no need to *demonstrate* adherence to the rule of law—it is taken as a given. This fact explains the divergence in public opinion between the prison abuse scandal in Iraq and the conditions in supermax prisons in the United States. Has anything happened at Abu Ghraib that would be unthinkable in a maximum-security prison in the United States? The sexual sadism, the humiliation, deprivation, humiliation? Charles Graner worked as a guard in a prison in the United States before being sent to Iraq. We can watch degradation and torture within our native penal system depicted in gruesome detail on cable television in shows such as *Oz*, but that is normalized within our own expectation of criminality and punishment in the United States. Many people have a fascination with the violence, sexual sadism, health problems, and denial of humanity involved in prison life in the United States. Reports of inmates being beaten to death, raped, dying from lack of health care, and even used in battles in Gladiator Days in California prisons are shocking, but routine. To then have the same group of people announce that they are appalled to find that such things happen in prisons run by the United States abroad is surprising indeed.

Whether the shock of seeing such displays of governmental power abroad will encourage American citizens to question what they take as a given at home remains to be seen. The audience of world opinion has certainly brought a new element to considerations of American practices of punishment, just as it did in More's utopian treatise. If pressure from Europe and China continues, extending from punitive practices abroad to those at home, we might see a renewed perception on the part of the America public that could spur reform.

The actions of the U.S. government and its agents in detaining suspects and torturing prisoners can be understood in no other terms except using punishment to demonstrate the power of command. Yet what distinguishes this demonstration of power is that the government is using punishment to create command over citizens of other countries. This surely exceeds the boundaries of what can be considered appropriate expressions of power. But these incidents also demonstrate why using state punishment to try to create the power of command is particularly disastrous. Just as Arendt explained, authority is strongest when it has no need to draw attention to itself or defend its exercise. Here, the U.S. government uses punishment to visibly and forcibly order what it experiences as a chaotic world, yet it only succeeds in creating ever more disorder.

This growing resistance to assertions of U.S. power means that I can end this book on an optimistic note, even though current policies offer little hope for immediate redemption. The promise of political order is a harmonious balance between the concentration of human capacities in the development of government and the circumscription of these powers by ideals and principles. History presents countless examples of regimes that have failed to maintain this balance, generally favoring the exercise of power over adherence to a set of ideals. It seems it is particularly tempting to violate this balance in conducting state punishment, as the recipients have so little power or sympathy. Abusing this prerogative has consistently disastrous effects for a regime, however. History shows that no political regime has been able to balance the requirements of power and justice perfectly, but it also demonstrates a persistent resistance to state injustice on the part of subjects. When states give in to the temptations of power and punish merely for the sake of command, punishment may sow obedience but will ultimately reap resistance.

Notes

Introduction

1. Marie Gottschalk, Mary Katzenstein, Stuart Scheingold, Bill Lyons, Jonathan Simon, David Garland, and Thomas Dumm have all conducted skillful and timely research into punishment and its politics. Political scientists have also extensively studied crime and "law and order" political behavior and electoral strategies. While these strategies may create support for the penal regime, these studies do not focus on the punishments that occur as a result of them. Disenfranchisement is also a new focus of concern among political scientists in the increasingly tight electoral map.

2. Max Weber, "Politics as a Vocation," in *From Max Weber* (New York: Taylor and Francis, 1948).

3. Here I have deliberately avoiding using the phrase "the state's subjects" because recent events demonstrate that one does not need to be a citizen or member of a polity to suffer punishment at the hands of its state.

4. My thanks to Daniel Tompkins for pointing this out.

5. Aristotle, *Nicomachean Ethics*, trans. Martin Oswald (Indianapolis: Bobbs-Merrill, 1962), 121.

6. G. F. W. Hegel, *Philosophy of Right*, trans. T. M. Knox (Oxford: Oxford University Press, 1952), 141.

7. Whether the law actually does this is of course a matter of debate. Some have argued that revenge has always lurked inside the law. Others argue that recent changes in victims' rights have reintroduced the element of revenge in the law (Culbert 2001). For a complete discussion, see Roger Berkowitz, "Revenge and Justice," *Journal of Law, Culture, and the Humanities* 1, no. 3 (2005).

8. Hegel, 70.

9. Philippe Nonet, "Sanction," *Cumberland Law Review* 25 (1995).

10. *Coppedge v. United States*, 369 U.S. 438.

11. *McCleskey v. Kemp*, 107 S. Ct. 1756 (1987).

Chapter 1

1. Judith Shklar, "The Political Theory of Utopia: From Melancholy to Nostalgia," in *Political Thought and Political Thinkers,* ed. Stanley Hoffman, 164, 165 (Chicago: University of Chicago Press, 1998).

2. Corey Robin, *Fear: The History of a Political Idea* (Oxford: Oxford University Press, 2004), 104.

3. George Kateb, "The Adequacy of the Canon," *Political Theory* 30, no. 4 (2002): 495.

4. I write about this issue extensively in *Collective Dreams: Political Imagination and Community* (University Park: Pennsylvania State University Press, 2005). See especially chap. 1, "The Politics of Imagination," and chap. 6, "Social Imagineering: Utopian Vision as Commodity Fetish."

5. Thomas More, *Utopia,* trans. Clarence H. Miller (New Haven: Yale University Press, 2001), 15.

6. Quentin Skinner, *The Foundation of Modern Political Thought* (Cambridge: Cambridge University Press, 1978), 218.

7. More, 19.

8. More, 25.

9. George M. Logan, *The Meaning of More's "Utopia"* (Princeton: Princeton University Press, 1983); "The Argument of Utopia," in *Interpreting Thomas More's "Utopia,"* ed. John C. Olin (New York: Fordham University Press, 1989).

10. More, 95–96.

11. More, 100.

12. Shlomo Avineri, "War and Slavery in More's *Utopia,*" *International Journal of Social History* 7 (1962): 288.

13. More, 44.

14. H. L. A. Hart, *Punishment and Responsibility: Essays in the Philosophy of Law* (Oxford: Oxford University Press, 1968), 23.

15. See Logan 1989, Skinner 1978, and Avineri 1962.

16. Gustav Janouch, *Conversations with Kafka,* trans. Goronwy Rees (New York: Praeger, 1953), 35.

17. Jane Bennett, "Kafka, Genealogy, and the Spiritualization of Politics," *Journal of Politics* 56, no. 3 (August 1994): 653.

18. Franz Kafka, "In the Penal Colony," *The Complete Stories* (New York: Schocken, 1971), 150. Quotations for this work are cited in the text.

19. Peter Neumeyer, "Franz Kafka, Sugar Baron," *Modern Fiction Studies* 17, no. 1 (Spring 1971): 11.

20. Walter Benjamin, *Illuminations,* ed. Hannah Arendt (New York: Harcourt Brace Jovanovich, 1969).

21. Arnold Weinstein, "Kafka's Writing Machine: Metamorphosis in the

Penal Colony," in *Critical Essays on Franz Kafka*, ed. Ruth V. Gross, 120–49 at 124 (Boston: G. K. Hall, 1990).

22. James Madison expressed frustration with this fact in Federalist 37: "But no language is so copious as to supply words and phrases for every complex idea, or so correct as not to include many, equivocally denoting different ideas. . . . When the Almighty himself condescends to address mankind in their own language, his meaning, luminous though it must be, is rendered dim and doubtful, by the cloudy medium through which it is communicated."

23. Sander Gilman, *Franz Kafka* (London: Reaktion Books, 2005).

24. Wilhelm Emrich, *Franz Kafka: A Critical Study of His Writings*, trans. Sheema Zeben Buehne (New York: Frederick Ungar, 1968).

25. Paul Peters, "Witness to the Execution: Kafka and Colonialism," *Monatshefte* 93, no. 4 (2001): 403.

26. Evelyn Torton Beck, *Kafka and the Yiddish Theater* (Madison: University of Wisconsin Press, 1971), and Erwin R. Steinberg, "The Judgment in Kafka's 'In the Penal Colony,'" *Journal of Modern Literature* 5, no. 3 (1976), see Jewish themes, and in Steinberg's case, formal failings, in the story. Martin Greenberg, *The Terror of Art: Kafka and Modern Literature* (New York: Basic Books, 1968) and Heinz Politzer, *Franz Kafka: Parable and Paradox* (Ithaca: Cornell University Press, 1966) see more Christian symbolism in the text.

27. Margaret Kohn, "Kafka's Critique of Colonialism," *Theory and Event* 8, no. 3 (2005); Karen Piper, "The Language of the Machine: A Postcolonial Reading of Kafka," *Journal of the Kafka Society of America* 20, no. 1–2 (1996): 42–54; Peters, "Witness to the Execution."

28. Peter Neumeyer (1971) examines a book that Kafka wrote was central to his life in 1914, Oskar Weber's *Der Zuckerbaron*, which recounts the life and adventures of a former German officer in South America. Strangely, the book closes with the officer imagining his own grave and inscription upon it, which is reminiscent of the ending of "In the Penal Colony." Anthony D. Northey conducted research into the activities of Kafka's uncles in colonial enterprises in "Kafka and Foreign Lands: The Life Stories of His Uncles," *Journal of the Kafka Society of America* 10, no. 1–2 (1986): 68–79.

29. Stephen A. Toth, "Colonisation or Incarceration?" *Journal of Pacific History* 34, no. 1 (June 1999).

30. Franz Kafka, "Jackals and Arabs," in *The Complete Stories*, ed. Nahum Glatzer, 407–10 (New York: Schocken, 1971). In this story, a "Northern European" traveling in what seems to be Egypt is recruited by a group of Jackals to prove his superior status by killing the Arabs for them. The Jackals seem to represent the settlers; the Arabs the native population; and the traveler once again represents the confused homeland trying to determine who is good and who is bad in an unfamiliar territory.

31. On January 26, 2006, Joshua Marquis, vice president of the National District Attorneys Association, published an editorial in the *New York Times* calculating a success rate of accurate convictions in the U.S. justice system at 99.973 percent. He comments, "Most industries would like to claim such a record of efficiency."

Chapter 2

1. Friedrich Nietzsche, *On the Genealogy of Morals,* trans. Walter Kaufman and R. J. Hollingdale (New York: Vintage, 1989), 67.

2. Thomas Hobbes, *Leviathan,* ed. Richard Tuck (Cambridge: Cambridge University Press, 1996), 93.

3. *The Book of Job,* trans. Stephen Mitchell (New York: Harper Perennial, 1992). Quotations for this work are cited in the text.

4. This reading is informed by Stephen Mitchell's excellent introduction to his translation.

5. See Aloysius Martinich, *The Two Gods of Leviathan: Thomas Hobbes on Religion and Politics* (New York: Cambridge University Press, 1992); A. E. Taylor, "The Ethical Doctrine of Hobbes," in *Hobbes; Studies, by Leo Strauss [and others],* ed. K. Brown (Cambridge: Harvard University Press, 1965); and Howard Warrender, *The Political Philosophy of Hobbes: His Theory of Obligation* (Oxford: Oxford University Press, 1957).

6. Arguments for Hobbes's nonbelief can be found in Quentin Skinner, *The Foundation of Modern Political Thought* (Cambridge: Cambridge University Press, 1978); Paul D. Cooke, *Hobbes and Christianity: Reassessing the Bible in Leviathan* (Lanham: Rowman and Littlefield, 1996), and his article "An Antidote to the Current Fashion of Regarding Hobbes as a Sincere Theist" in *Piety and Humanity,* ed. D. Kries, 79–108 (Lanham: Rowman and Littlefield, 1997), and also in Greg Forster, "Divine Law and Human Law in Hobbes's Leviathan," *History of Political Thought* 24:2003.

7. Deborah Baumgold, *Hobbes's Political Theory* (Cambridge: Cambridge University Press, 1988), 120.

8. W. H. Greenleaf, "A Note on Hobbes and the Book of Job," *Anales de la Catedra Francisco Suarez* 14 (1974): 11–34 at 14.

9. Greenleaf, "A Note on Hobbes," 33–34.

10. R. J. Halliday, Timothy Kenyon, and Andrew Reeve, "Hobbes's Belief in God," *Political Studies* 31 (1983): 433.

11. Michael Oakeshott, Introduction, *Leviathan* (Oxford: Basil Blackwell, 1946), xx.

12. Hobbes, *Leviathan,* 76. Additional citations to this work are given in the text.

13. Mitchell, *Book of Job,* 14.

14. Richard Tuck, *Philosophy and Government, 1572–1651* (Cambridge: Cambridge University Press, 1993), 279–314.

15. Tuck, *Philosophy and Government*, 286.

16. See D. S. T. Clark, *Vanities of the Eye: Vision in European Cultural Debate, 1425–1680* (Oxford: Oxford University Press, 2007).

17. Albert Camus, *The Myth of Sisyphus and Other Essays* (New York: Random House, 1955), 89–90.

18. Camus, *Myth of Sisyphus*, 91.

Chapter 3

1. Giorgio Agamben looks at sovereignty and the growth of power in *Homo Sacer: Sovereign Power and Bare Life*, trans. Daniel Heller-Roazen (Stanford: Stanford University Press, 1998), and at the state of emergency and sovereignty in contemporary politics in *State of Exception*, trans. Kevin Attell (Chicago: University of Chicago Press, 2005). Michael Hardt and Antonio Negri examine the evolution of sovereignty in *Empire* (Cambridge: Cambridge University Press, 2000). Michel Foucault's recently translated and published lectures, *"Society Must Be Defended": Lectures at the Collège de France, 1975–1976*, trans. David Macey, ed. Mauro Bertani and Alessandro Fontana (New York: Picador Press, 2003), also contain an extended discussion of political sovereignty, though his earlier published work "Governmentality" in *The Foucault Effect: Studies in Governmentality*, ed. Graham Burchell, Colin Gordon, and Peter Miller (London: Harvester Wheatsheaf, 1991) and *Discipline and Punish: The Birth of the Prison*, trans. Alan Sheridan (New York: Vintage, 1977) also examine the topic. There has also been a renewed interest in the work of Carl Schmitt, *Political Theology: Four Chapters on the Concept of Sovereignty*, trans. George Schwab (Cambridge: MIT Press, 1985), and Walter Benjamin's "Critique of Violence," in *Reflections: Essays, Aphorisms, and Autobiographical Writings*, ed. Peter Demetz and trans. Edmund Jephcott (New York: Schocken, 1978), both of which were key texts in earlier debates about the character of sovereignty and law.

2. Hardt and Negri, 84.

3. Plowden, 212a, 1816, cited in Ernst H. Kantorowicz's *The King's Two Bodies: A Study in Medieval Political Theology* (Princeton: Princeton University Press, 1957), 7.

4. Foucault, "Governmentality," 95.

5. John Austin, *Province of Jurisprudence Determined* (New York: Humanities Press, 1965), 301.

6. Austin, 194.

7. Charles Merriam, *History of the Theory of Sovereignty since Rousseau* (New York: Garland, 1972), 149.

8. Foucault, "Governmentality," 91.

9. R. W. K. Hinton, "Bodin and the Retreat into Legalism," *Proceedings of the International Conference on Bodin in München,* ed. Horst Denzer, 310 (Munich: C. H. Beck, 1973).

10. Bodin, *On Sovereignty,* ed. and trans. Julian Franklin, 23 (Cambridge: Cambridge University Press, 1992).

11. Foucault, *"Society Must Be Defended,"* 37.

12. Foucault, *"Society Must Be Defended,"* 17.

13. Schmitt, 36.

14. Schmitt, 12.

15. Schmitt, 13.

16. Foucault, *Discipline and Punish,* 48.

17. Foucault, "Governmentality," 103.

18. See Robert Gordon, "Popular Justice," in *Companion to the Anthropology of Politics,* ed. D. Nugent and J. Vincent (Malden: Blackwells, 2004), and Jean Comaroff and John Comaroff, "Criminal Obsessions, After Foucault: Postcoloniality, Policing, and the Metaphysics of Disorder" *Critical Inquiry* 30, no. 4 (2004): 800–825.

19. Albert Camus, *The Myth of Sisyphus and Other Essays* (New York: Random House, 1955), 175.

20. Henry David Thoreau, "Civil Disobedience," in *Political Thought in the United States: A Documentary History,* ed. Lynn Tower Sargent, 214 (New York: New York University Press, 1997).

Chapter 4

1. *Roper v. Simmons,* 543 U.S. 551 (2005).

2. The Society for Political Enquiries could be considered the first American Political Science Association. The members met at Benjamin Franklin's house to discuss the science of law, government, and the connection between political institutions and public morality. Members could write papers, submit them to the president and vice president for approval, and then present them for discussion at meetings. Thomas Paine wrote the charter from which the preceding passage is taken. The society is still intact today. Early documents are housed at the American Philosophical Society, Philadelphia.

3. George Rusche and Otto Kirschheimer, *Punishment and Social Structure* (New York: Columbia University Press, 1939).

4. William Bradford, "An Inquiry How Far the Punishment of Death Is Necessary in Pennsylvania,"American Philosophical Society Archives, 1793, 5.

5. Thomas Jefferson, *The Life and Selected Writings of Thomas Jefferson,* ed. Adrienne Koch and William Peden, 488, 491 (New York: Random House, 1944).

6. Rusche and Kirschheimer, 55.

7. Rusche and Kirschheimer, 53.

8. A. E. Smith, *Colonists in Bondage: White Servitude and Convict Labour in America, 1607–1776* (Baltimore: Clearfield, 2000).

9. Transportation Act 1717. *Statutes at Large, from Magna Charta to 1761*, vol. 5, carefully collated and revised by Danby Pickering (Cambridge, 1762).

10. Different crimes were given different categorizations according to religious doctrine, an element of the criminal law remaining from the Middle Ages.

11. Roger A. Ekrich, *Bound for America: The Transportation of British Convicts to the Colonies, 1718–1775* (Oxford: Clarendon, 1987).

12. Smith, *Colonists in Bondage*.

13. Benjamin Balak and Jonathan M. Lave, "The Dismal Science of Punishment: The Legal-Economy of Convict Transportation to the American Colonies," manuscript, 2002.

14. Balak and Lave, "Dismal Science."

15. Jeremy Bentham, "A Comparative View of the System of Penal Colonization in New South Wales and the Home Penitentiary System," pamphlet presented to the Lord Chancellor (American Philosophical Library, 1802); and Balak and Lave, "Dismal Science."

16. Smith, *Colonists in Bondage*.

17. Lord Beauchamp, "Recommendations for the Disposal of Convicts," *Commons Journal* 40:1161–64.

18. According to one national, Rob Gordon, transport never happened to Namibia because "water was even scarcer than gin."

19. "Pitt Government's Plan for Botany Bay Settlement" 1786.

20. Bentham 1802, 38.

21. Bentham 1802, 6.

22. The pamphlet is in the archives of the American Philosophical Society, with the handwritten message "To Caleb Lownes—From Jeremy Bentham."

23. Bernard Bailyn, *The Ideological Origins of the American Revolution* (Cambridge: Harvard University Press, 1967).

24. James Heath, *Eighteenth Century Penal Theory* (Oxford: Oxford University Press, 1963).

25. Cesare Beccaria, *On Crimes and Punishments and Other Writings*, ed. Richard Bellamy and trans. Richard Davies (Cambridge: Cambridge University Press, 1995), 70–71.

26. See the introductory essay by Richard Bellamy in Beccaria, *On Crimes and Punishments*, and Adolph Caso, *America's Italian Founding Fathers* (Boston: Brandon Press, 1975).

27. Foucault, *Discipline and Punish: The Birth of the Prison*, trans. Alan Sheridan (New York: Vintage, 1977), 110.

28. Beccaria, 68.

29. Beccaria, 87.

30. Beccaria, 69.

31. Negley Teeters, *The Cradle of the Penitentiary: The Walnut Street Jail at Philadelphia, 1793–1835* (Pennsylvania Prison Society, 1955), and Michael Meranze, *Laboratories of Virtue: Punishment, Revolution, and Authority in Philadelphia, 1760–1835* (Chapel Hill: University of North Carolina Press, 1996) have published the most complete historical studies of the Walnut Street Jail.

32. Teeters, 21.

33. Today this is Washington Square Park, a lovely spot in the middle of the historical tourist destinations of colonial Philadelphia.

34. Bradford, 20.

35. Pennsylvania Constitution of 1776.

36. Teeters, 27.

37. Rush, "An Inquiry into the Effects of Public Punishments Upon Criminals and Society." Delivered at the Society for Political Enquiries, 1787, American Philosophical Society Library, 14.

38. Robert J. Turnbull, "A Visit to the Philadelphia Prison" (Philadelphia: Budd and Betram, 1796), 50.

39. Turnbull, 48.

40. Turnbull, 58–59.

41. Reprinted in Teeters.

Chapter 5

1. Bruce Western, *Punishment and Inequality in America*, chap. 1 (New York: Russell Sage Foundation, 2006).

2. Western, *Punishment and Inequality in America*, Marie Gottschalk, *The Prison and the Gallows* (Cambridge: Cambridge University Press, 2006), David Garland, and Loic Wocquant are just a few of the researchers who make comprehensive arguments about the source of the incarceration boom.

3. See Herbert Morris, "Persons and Punishment," in *Monist* 52, no. 4 (1968): 475–501, for the classic articulation of this argument.

4. C. S. Nino, "A Consensual Theory of Punishment," *Philosophy and Public Affairs* 12 (1983): 289–306. Critics of this argument include T. Honderich, *Punishment: The Supposed Justifications* (New York: Penguin, 1988), and L. Alexander, "Consent, Punishment, and Proportionality," *Philosophy and Public Affairs* 15 (1986): 178–82.

5. See W. D. Ross, *The Right and the Good* (Oxford: Clarendon, 1965), 56–64.

6. Two excellent sources that reflect more recent debates about the philosophical justifications of punishment in a liberal framework are R. A. Duff and David Garland, Introduction, in *A Reader on Punishment* (Oxford: Oxford University Press, 1994), and a collection edited by Matt Matravers, *Punishment and Political Theory* (Oxford: Hart, 1999).

7. Carole Pateman, *The Sexual Contract* (Stanford: Stanford University Press, 1988); Jennifer Pitts, *The Turn to Empire* (Princeton: Princeton University Press, 2005); and Uday Singh Mehta, *Liberalism and Empire: A Study in Nineteenth Century British Liberal Thought* (Chicago: University of Chicago Press, 1999).

8. John Locke, *An Essay Concerning Human Understanding* (New York: Dover, 1959), 467.

9. Locke, *Essay*, 459.

10. Locke, *Essay*, 463n2.

11. Locke, *Essay*, 461.

12. H. L. A. Hart, *Punishment and Responsibility: Essays in the Philosophy of Law* (Oxford: Oxford University Press, 1968), 46.

13. Hugo Grotius, *De Jure Belli ac Pacis*, trans. Francis W. Kelsey (Oxford: Clarendon, 1925), 465.

14. Locke, *Essay*, 474.

15. Locke, *Two Treatises of Government*, ed. Peter Laslett, 271 (Cambridge: Cambridge University Press, 1988).

16. Locke, *Two Treatises*, 272.

17. Hugo Grotius, *De Jure Praedae Commentarius*, trans. G. L. Williams and Walter Zeydel (Oxford: Clarendon, 1950), 91–92.

18. Locke, *Two Treatises*, 273.

19. Grotius, *De Jure Belli*, 468–69.

20. Locke, *Two Treatises*, 272.

21. Locke, "A Second Letter Concerning Toleration" from *The Works of John Locke in Nine Volumes*, vol. 5, 100. 12th ed. (London: Rivington, 1824).

22. Robert Nozick, *Anarchy, State, and Utopia* (New York: Basic Books, 1974).

23. Grotius, *De Jure Praedae Commentarius*, 94.

24. Locke, *Second Treatise*, 401.

25. Locke, *Second Treatise*, 400.

26. See Roger Berkowitz, ed., "Revenge and Justice," *Journal of Law, Culture, and Humanities* 1, no. 3 (2005), and Jennifer L. Culbert, "The Sacred Name of Pain: The Role of Victim Impact Evidence in Death Penalty Sentencing Decisions," in *Pain, Death, and the Law*, ed. Austin Sarat (Ann Arbor: University of Michigan Press, 2001), for examples of this argument. Others argue that victims' rights groups have succeeded in reintroducing the principle of revenge into American courts. Certainly forms of community justice would be vulnerable to the impulse for revenge, though evidence is mixed as to whether this actually occurs.

27. Locke, *Second Treatise*, 415.

28. Jeremy Bentham, *A Fragment on Government*, ed. J. H. Burns and H. L. A. Hart (Cambridge: Cambridge University Press, 1988), 52.

29. Wilfred Harrison, "Introduction," in Jeremy Bentham, *A Fragment on Government and An Introduction to the Principles of Morals and Legislation*, ed. Wilfred Harrison (Oxford: B. Blackwell, 1967), xvii.

30. Bentham, *Fragment*, 52.

31. Bentham, *Fragment*, 108, emphasis in original.

32. Jeremy Bentham, *An Introduction to the Principles of Morals and Legislation*, ed. J. H. Burns and H. L. A. Hart, 11 (Oxford: Clarendon, 1996).

33. H. L. A. Hart, *Essays on Bentham: Jurisprudence and Political Theory* (Oxford: Oxford University Press, 1982), and Philip Schofield, "Political and Religious Radicalism in the Thought of Jeremy Bentham," *History of Political Thought* 20, no. 2 (1000): 272–91.

34. Jeremy Bentham, "Fragment on Ontology," *The Works of Jeremy Bentham*, ed. John Bowring, vol. 8, 197 (Edinburgh: William Tait, 1843).

35. Bentham, "Ontology."

36. Bentham, "Ontology," 210–11.

37. Bentham, "Ontology," 206.

38. Bentham, *Fragment*, 11.

39. David Garland, *The Culture of Control* (Chicago: University of Chicago Press, 2001). See especially chapter 8.

40. Marie Gottschalk, *The Prison and the Gallows: The Politics of Mass Incarceration in America* (Cambridge: Cambridge University Press, 2006). See her introduction and chapters 5, 6, and 7 for her new analysis of the role of interest groups in recent mass incarceration in the United States.

Chapter 6

1. John Locke, *Two Treatises of Government*, ed. Peter Laslett (Cambridge: Cambridge University Press, 1988).

2. Nancy Hirschmann, "Liberal Conservatism, Once and Again," *Constellations* 9, no. 3 (2002): 340.

3. Locke, *Two Treatises*, 322–23.

4. Judith Shklar, *American Citizenship: The Quest for Inclusion* (Cambridge: Harvard University Press, 1991).

5. Alice Kessler-Harris, *In Pursuit of Equity: Women, Men, and the Quest for Economic Citizenship in Twentieth Century America* (Oxford: Oxford University Press, 2001), 4.

6. Kessler-Harris, *In Pursuit of Equity*, 4.

7. See Nancy Fraser and Linda Gordon, "'A Genealogy of 'Dependency': Tracing a Keyword of the U.S. Welfare State," in Nancy Fraser, *Justice Interruptus* (New York: Routledge, 1997); Gwendolyn Mink, *Welfare's End* (Ithaca: Cornell University Press, 1998); and Frank Munger, "Dependency by Law: Welfare and Identity in the Lives of Poor Women," in *Lives in the Law*, ed. Austin Sarat, Lawrence Douglas, and Martha Merrill Umphrey (Ann Arbor: University of Michigan Press, 2002), 83–121. Debates about immigration in 2006 suggest that we may be entering a new era, when work and citizenship are not tied together.

8. Jonathan Simon and Malcolm Feeley, "True Crime: The New Penology and the Public Discourse on Crime," in *Punishment and Social Control*, ed. T. Blomberg and S. Cohen (New York: Aldine de Gruyter, 1995), 150.

9. David Garland, *The Culture of Control* (Chicago: University of Chicago Press, 2001), 47.

10. *Ruffin v. The Commonwealth*, 62 Va. 1024. Nov. 1871.

11. Joan Dayan, "Held in the Body of the State," in *History, Memory, and the Law*, ed. Austin Sarat and Thomas R. Kearns (Ann Arbor: University of Michigan Press, 1999).

12. See Christopher Uggen and Jeff Manza, "Democratic Contraction? Political Consequences of Felon Disenfranchisement in the United States," *American Sociological Review* 67 (2002): 777–803. They present the different franchise restrictions currently in place and speculate how re-enfranchisement could change electoral politics.

13. Alex Lichtenstein, *Twice the Work of Free Labor: The Political Economy of Convict Labor in the New South* (New York: Verso, 1996).

14. Stanley Engerman, "The Economic Response to Emancipation and Some Economic Aspects of the Meaning of Freedom," in *The Meaning of Freedom*, ed. F. McGlynn (Pittsburgh: University of Pittsburgh Press, 1992), 49–68.

15. Lichtenstein, 13.

16. Lichtenstein, 30.

17. Eric Foner, *Free Soil, Free Labor, Free Men: The Ideology of the Republican Party* (New York: Oxford University Press, 1970), 46.

18. Morgan Reynolds, "The Economic Impact of Prison Labor," National Center for Policy Analysis, 1997; Christian Parenti, "Making Prison Pay," *Nation* 262, no. 4 (1996): 11–14.

19. Bureau of Prisons, Official Information, 2002.

20. Christian Parenti, *Lockdown America: Police and Prisons in the Age of Crisis* (New York: Verso, 1999), 232.

21. Parenti, *Lockdown America*, 233.

22. Philadelphia Prison System Annual Report, 2001, 15.

23. Morgan Reynolds and Knut Rostad, "Creating Factories behind Bars," National Center for Policy Analysis, Brief 354, 2001 (available at http://www.ncpa.org/pub/ba/ba354/). In spring 2006, it was suggested during the debate about immigration reform and labor shortages that convicts in California's penal system could take over the labor requirements for agriculture in the state.

24. Reynolds and Rostad, "Creating Factories behind Bars."

25. House Judiciary Committee, Subcommittee on Crime, "Prison Industry Reform Legislation," 105th Cong., 2d sess., June 25, 1998, 63.

26. Troy Duster, "Postindustrialism and Youth Unemployment in the US," in *Poverty, Inequality, and the Future of Social Policy: Western States in the New*

World Order, ed. K. McFate, R. Lawson, and W. J. Wilson, 474 (New York: Russell Sage Foundation, 1995).

27. See Duster, "Postindustrialism and Youth Unemployment," and also Saskia Sassen, *Globalization and Its Discontents* (New York: Free Press, 1998), for arguments about the fate of minorities and patterns of deindustrialization.

28. Philadelphia Prison System Fiscal Year Report 2001.

29. Bruce Western and Katherine Beckett, "How Unregulated Is the U.S. Labor Market? The Penal System as a Labor Market Institution," *American Journal of Sociology* 104, no. 4 (1999): 1030–60. See also Western's *Punishment and Inequality in Amerca* (New York: Sage, 2006).

30. Jonathan Simon, *Poor Discipline* (Chicago: University of Chicago Press, 1993), 164.

31. Simon, 265.

32. Alexis de Tocqueville and Gustave de Beaumont, *The Penitentiary System in the United States and Its Application in France* (New York: Augustus Kelley, 1970), 57.

33. Thomas Dumm, *Democracy and Punishment: The Disciplinary Origins of the United States* (Madison: University of Wisconsin Press, 1987).

34. See Parenti, *Lockdown America,* and Joseph Hallinan, *Going Up the River: Travels in a Prison Nation* (New York: Random House, 2001) for vivid accounts of nightmarish conditions in supermax facilities today.

35. David Theo Goldberg, "Surplus Value: The Political Economy of Prisons and Policing," in *States of Confinement: Policing, Detentions, and Prisons,* ed. Joy James, 215 (New York: St. Martin's, 2000).

36. Foucault, *Discipline and Punish: The Birth of the Prison,* trans. Alan Sheridan (New York: Vintage, 1977), 208.

37. Parenti, "Making Prison Pay."

38. David Steves, "As Many Oregonians Lose Work, Prisons Add Inmate Jobs," *Register Guard,* December 24, 2001.

39. Both Dayan and Hallinan describe this practice.

40. Albert Camus, "The Myth of Sisyphus," in *The Myth of Sisyphus and Other Essays* (New York: Random House, 1955), 89–90.

41. Tocqueville and Beaumont, 157.

Chapter 7

1. Arendt, "On Violence," in *Crises of the Republic* (New York: Harcourt Brace Jovanovich, 1973), 155.

2. Arendt, 144.

3. Arendt, 144.

4. Arendt, 152.

5. Friedrich Nietzsche, *On the Genealogy of Morals,* trans. Walter Kaufman and R. J. Hollingdale (New York: Vintage, 1989), 72.

6. Arendt, 151.

7. Emma Goldman, "Prisons: A Social Crime and Failure," in *Anarchism and Other Essays* (New York: Dover Publications, 1969), 109–26.

8. This position appears to be at the bottom of recent U.S. policies. Jane Mayer examined the philosophical outlook of David Addington, Vice President Cheney's Chief of Staff and one of the legal minds behind administration policies. He believes that legality is secondary to executive authority and therefore all executive actions are beyond question. See Jane Mayer, "The Hidden Power," *New Yorker* 82, no. 20 (2006): 44–55.

9. The *New York Times* published an article on March 19, 2006, revealing practices of abuse at Camp Nama, a location near the Baghdad airport where even more egregious acts were committed against detainees. It seems that this list could keep growing, as human rights organizations are interviewing those who have been detained. They claim that there are dozens of places in Iraq—thus far without names—where U.S. soldiers have been abusing, killing, and raping detainees.

10. "China Hits Back at US Criticism," BBC News International Version, March 9, 2006.

11. Karen Greenberg and Joshua Dratel, eds., *The Torture Papers: The Road to Abu Ghraib* (Cambridge: Cambridge University Press, 2005), 520.

12. Greenberg and Dratel, 484.

13. Greenberg and Dratel, 466.

14. United Nations, Economic and Social Council, Commission on Human Rights, "Situation of Detainees at Guantanamo Bay," report released February 15, 2006.

15. This is Giorgio Agamben's argument in *State of Exception.*

16. UN, "Situation of Detainees." In response to this report, Vice President Cheney declared that it was "an embarrassment to the United Nations." February 16, 2006.

17. BBC, "Guantanamo Interview: Full Transcript." March 3, 2006. http://news.bbc.co.uk/2/hi/americas/4770390.stm.

18. Niccolò Machiavelli, *The Prince and the Discourses* (New York: Modern Library, 1950), 27.

19. *New York Times*, May 12, 2005.

20. *New York Times*, June 22, 2004.

References

Agamben, Giorgio. 1998. *Homo Sacer: Sovereign Power and Bare Life.* Trans. Daniel Heller-Roazen. Stanford: Stanford University Press.

———. 2005. *State of Exception.* Trans. Kevin Attell. Chicago: University of Chicago Press.

Alexander, L. 1986. "Consent, Punishment, and Proportionality." *Philosophy and Public Affairs* 15:178–82.

Arendt, Hannah. 1973. *Crises of the Republic.* New York: Harcourt Brace Jovanovich.

Aristotle. 1962. *Nicomachean Ethics.* Trans. Martin Oswald. Indianapolis: Bobbs-Merrill.

Austin, John. [1832] 1965. *The Province of Jurisprudence Determined.* New York: Humanities Press.

Avineri, Shlomo. 1962. "War and Slavery in More's *Utopia.*" *International Journal of Social History* 7:260–90.

Bailyn, Bernard. 1967. *The Ideological Origins of the American Revolution.* Cambridge: Harvard University Press.

Balak, Benjamin, and Jonathan M. Lave. 2002. "The Dismal Science of Punishment: The Legal-Economy of Convict Transportation to the American Colonies." Manuscript.

Baumgold, Deborah. 1988. *Hobbes's Political Theory.* Cambridge: Cambridge University Press.

Beauchamp, Lord. 1785. "Recommendations for the Disposal of Convicts." *Commons Journals* 40:1161–64.

Beccaria, Cesare. 1995. *On Crimes and Punishments and Other Writings.* Ed. Richard Bellamy and trans. Richard Davies. Cambridge: Cambridge University Press.

Beck, Evelyn Torton. 1971. *Kafka and Yiddish Theater.* Madison: University of Wisconsin Press.

Benjamin, Walter. 1969. *Illuminations.* Ed. Hannah Arendt. New York: Harcourt Brace Jovanovich.

———. 1978. "Critique of Violence." *Reflections: Essays, Aphorisms, Autobiographical Writings.* Ed. Peter Demetz and trans. Edmund Jephcott. New York: Schocken.

Bennett, Jane. 1994. "Kafka, Genealogy, and the Spiritualization of Politics." *Journal of Politics* 56, no. 3: 650–70.

Bentham, Jeremy. 1802. "A Comparative View of the System of Penal Colonization in New South Wales and the Home Penitentiary System." Pamphlet presented to the Lord Chancellor. In American Philosophical Society Library.

———. 1843. "Fragment on Ontology." *The Works of Jeremy Bentham.* Ed. John Bowring. Vol. 8, 193–211. Edinburgh: William Tait.

———. 1988. *A Fragment on Government.* Ed. J. H. Burns and H. L. A. Hart. Cambridge: Cambridge University Press. Epigraph for chapter 5, this vol., at 52.

———. 1996. *An Introduction to the Principles of Morals and Legislation.* Ed. J. H. Burns and H. L. A. Hart. Oxford: Clarendon.

Berkowitz, Roger, ed. 2005. "Revenge and Justice." *Journal of Law, Culture, and the Humanities* 1, no. 3.

Bodin, Jean. 1992. *On Sovereignty.* Ed. and trans. Julian Franklin. Cambridge: Cambridge University Press.

Bradford, William. 1793. "An Enquiry How Far the Punishment of Death Is Necessary in Pennsylvania." American Philosophical Society library.

Camus, Albert. 1955. *The Myth of Sisyphus and Other Essays.* New York: Random House.

Caso, Adolph. 1975. *America's Italian Founding Fathers.* Boston: Branden Press.

Clark, D. S. T. Forthcoming. *Vanities of the Eye: Vision in European Cultural Debate, 1425–1680.* Oxford: Oxford University Press.

Comaroff, Jean, and John Comaroff. 2004. "Criminal Obsessions, After Foucault: Postcoloniality, Policing, and the Metaphysics of Disorder." *Critical Inquiry* 30, no. 4: 800–825.

Cooke, Paul D. 1996. *Hobbes and Christianity: Reassessing the Bible in "Leviathan."* Lanham, MD: Rowman and Littlefield.

———. 1997. "An Antidote to the Current Fashion of Regarding Hobbes as a Sincere Theist." In *Piety and Humanity,* ed. D. Kries, 79–108. Lanham, MD: Rowman and Littlefield.

Culbert, Jennifer L. 2001. "The Sacred Name of Pain: The Role of Victim Impact Evidence in Death Penalty Sentencing Decisions." In *Pain, Death, and the Law,* ed. Austin Sarat. Ann Arbor: University of Michigan Press.

Dayan, Joan. 1999. "Held in the Body of the State." In *History, Memory, and the Law,* ed. Austin Sarat and Thomas R. Kearns. Ann Arbor: University of Michigan Press.

Duff, R. A., and David Garland. 1994. Introduction. In *A Reader on Punishment.* Oxford: Oxford University Press.

Dumm, Thomas L. 1987. *Democracy and Punishment: The Disciplinary Origins of the United States.* Madison: University of Wisconsin Press.

Duster, Troy. 1995. "Postindustrialism and Youth Unemployment in the US." In *Poverty, Inequality, and the Future of Social Policy: Western States in the New World Order,* ed. K. McFate, R. Lawson, and W. J. Wilson. New York: Russell Sage Foundation.

Ekrich, Roger A. 1987. *Bound for America: The Transportation of British Convicts to the Colonies, 1718–1775.* Oxford: Clarendon.

Emrich, Wilhelm. 1968. *Franz Kafka: A Critical Study of His Writings.* Trans. Sheema Zeben Buehne. New York: Frederick Ungar.

Engerman, Stanley. 1992. "The Economic Response to Emancipation and Some Economic Aspects of the Meaning of Freedom." In *The Meaning of Freedom,* ed. F. McGlynn, 49–68. Pittsburgh: University of Pittsburgh Press.

Farrell, Daniel. 1988. "Punishment Without the State." *Noûs* 22, no. 3: 437–53.

Fitzpatrick, Peter. 2001. *Modernism and the Grounds of Law.* Cambridge: Cambridge University Press.

Foner, Eric. 1970. *Free Soil, Free Labor, Free Men: The Ideology of the Republican Party.* New York: Oxford University Press.

Forster, Greg. 2003. "Divine Law and Human Law in Hobbes's Leviathan." *History of Political Thought* 24 (Summer): 189–217.

Foucault, Michel. 1977. *Discipline and Punish: The Birth of the Prison.* Trans. Alan Sheridan. New York: Vintage Books.

———. 1991. *The Foucault Effect: Studies in Governmentality.* Ed. Graham Burchell, Colin Gordon, and Peter Miller. London: Harvester Wheatsheaf.

———. 2003. *"Society Must Be Defended": Lectures at the Collège de France, 1975–1976.* Trans. David Macey and ed. Mauro Bertani and Alessandro Fontana. New York: Picador.

Fraser, Nancy, and Linda Gordon. 1997. "A Genealogy of 'Dependency': Tracing a Keyword of the U.S. Welfare State." In *Justice Interruptus,* Nancy Fraser. New York: Routledge.

Freud, Sigmund. 1960. *Totem and Taboo.* Trans. James Strachey. London: Routledge and Kegan Paul.

Garland, David. 2001. *The Culture of Control.* Chicago: University of Chicago Press.

Gilman, Sander. 2005. *Franz Kafka.* London: Reaktion Books.

Goldberg, David Theo. 2000. "Surplus Value: The Political Economy of Prisons and Policing." In *States of Confinement: Policing, Detentions, and Prisons,* ed. J. James. New York: St. Martin's Press.

Goldman, Alan H. "The Paradox of Punishment." *Philosophy and Public Affairs* 9, no. 1: 42–58.

Goldman, Emma. 1969. "Prisons: A Social Crime and Failure." In *Anarchism and Other Essays,* 109–26. New York: Dover.

Gordon, Robert J. 2004. " Popular Justice." In *Companion to the Anthropology of Politics*, ed. D. Nugent and J. Vincent, 349–66. Malden: Blackwells.

Gottschalk, Marie. 2006. *The Prison and the Gallows: The Politics of Mass Incarceration in America*. Cambridge: Cambridge University Press.

Greenberg, Karen J., and Joshua Dratel, eds. 2005. *The Torture Papers: The Road to Abu Ghraib*. Cambridge: Cambridge University Press.

Greenberg, Martin. 1968. *The Terror of Art: Kafka and Modern Literature*. New York: Basic Books.

Greenleaf, W. H. 1974. "A Note on Hobbes and the Book of Job." *Anales de la Catedra Francisco Suarez* 14:11–34.

Grotius, Hugo. 1925. *De Jure Belli ac Pacis*. Trans. Francis W. Kelsey, 462–521. Oxford: Clarendon.

———. 1950. *De Jure Praedae Commentarius*. Trans. G. L. Williams and Walter Zeydel. Oxford: Clarendon.

Halliday, R. J., Timothy Kenyon, and Andrew Reeve. 1983. "Hobbes's Belief in God." *Political Studies* 31:418–33.

Hallinan, Joseph T. 2001. *Going Up the River: Travels in a Prison Nation*. New York: Random House.

Hardt, Michael, and Antonio Negri. 2000. *Empire*. Cambridge: Harvard University Press.

Harrison, Wilfred. 1967. "Introduction" to Jeremy Bentham, *A Fragment on Government and An Introduction to the Principles of Morals and Legislation*, ed. W. Harrison. Oxford: B. Blackwell.

Hart, H. L. A. 1968. *Punishment and Responsibility: Essays in the Philosophy of Law*. Oxford: Oxford University Press.

———. 1982. *Essays on Bentham: Jurisprudence and Political Theory*. Oxford: Oxford University Press.

Heath, James. 1963. *Eighteenth Century Penal Theory*. Oxford: Oxford University Press.

Hegel, G. F. W. 1952. *Philosophy of Right*. Trans. T. M. Knox. Oxford: Oxford University Press.

Hinton, R. W. K. 1973. "Bodin and the Retreat into Legalism." *Proceedings of the International Conference on Bodin in München*, ed. Horst Denzer, 303–13. Munich: C. H. Beck.

Hirschmann, Nancy. 2002. "Liberal Conservatism, Once and Again." *Constellations* 9, no. 3: 335–55.

Hobbes, Thomas. 1996. *Leviathan*. Ed. Richard Tuck. Cambridge: Cambridge University Press.

Honderich, T. 1988. *Punishment: The Supposed Justifications*. New York: Penguin.

Hubbell, Webb. 2000. "Without Pardon: Collateral Consequences of a Felony Conviction." *Federal Sentencing Reporter* 13, no. 3–4: 223–24.

Jackson, Shirley. 1982. *The Lottery and Other Stories*. New York: Farrar, Straus and Giroux.

Janouch, Gustave. 1953. *Conversations with Kafka*. Trans. Goronwy Rees. New York: Praeger.

Jefferson, Thomas. 1944. *The Life and Selected Writings of Thomas Jefferson*. Ed. Adrienne Koch and William Peden. New York: Random House.

Kafka, Franz. 1971. "In the Penal Colony" and "Jackals and Arabs." Trans. Willa Muir and Edwin Muir. In *The Complete Stories*, ed. Nahum Glatzer. New York: Schocken.

———. 2001. *The Trial*. New York: Schocken Books.

Kantorowicz, Ernst H. 1957. *The King's Two Bodies: A Study in Medieval Political Theology*. Princeton: Princeton University Press.

Kateb, George. 2002. "The Adequacy of the Canon." *Political Theory* 30, no. 4: 482–505.

Kaufman-Osborn, Timothy. 2001. "What the Law Must Not Hear: On Capital Punishment and the Voice of Pain." In *Pain, Death, and the Law*, ed. Austin Sarat. Ann Arbor: University of Michigan Press.

Kessler-Harris, Alice. 2001. *In Pursuit of Equity: Women, Men, and the Quest for Economic Citizenship in Twentieth Century America*. Oxford: Oxford University Press.

Kohn, Margaret. 2005. "Kafka's Critique of Colonialism." *Theory and Event* 8, no. 3.

Levinson, Sanford, ed. 2004. *Torture: A Collection*. Oxford: Oxford University Press.

Lichtenstein, Alex. 1996. *Twice the Work of Free Labor: The Political Economy of Convict Labor in the New South*. New York: Verso.

Locke, John. 1824. "A Second Letter Concerning Toleration." In *The Works of John Locke in Nine Volumes*, vol. 5. 12th ed. London: Rivington.

———. 1959. *An Essay Concerning Human Understanding*. Vol. 1. New York: Dover.

———. 1988. *Two Treatises of Government*. Ed. Peter Laslett. Cambridge: Cambridge University Press.

Logan, George M. 1983. *The Meaning of More's "Utopia."* Princeton: Princeton University Press.

———. 1989. "The Argument of Utopia." In *Interpreting Thomas More's "Utopia,"* ed. John C. Olin, 7–35. New York: Fordham University Press.

Lownes, Caleb. 1793. "An Account of the Gaol and Penitentiary House of Philadelphia, and of the Interior Management Thereof." American Philosophical Society library.

Machiavelli, Niccolò. 1950. *The Prince and the Discourses*. New York: Modern Library.

Marquis, Joshua. 2006. Editorial. *New York Times*. January 26.

Martinich, Aloysius. 1992. *The Two Gods of Leviathan: Thomas Hobbes on Religion and Politics*. New York: Cambridge University Press.

Matravers, Matt. 1999. *Punishment and Political Theory*. Oxford: Hart.

Mayer, Jane. 2006. "The Hidden Power." *New Yorker* 82, no. 20: 44–55.

McBride, Keally. 2005. *Collective Dreams: Political Imagination and Community.* University Park: Pennsylvania State University Press.

Meastro, Marcello. 1973. *Cesare Beccaria and the Origins of Penal Reform.* Philadelphia: Temple University Press.

Mehta, Uday Singh. 1999. *Liberalism and Empire: A Study in Nineteenth Century British Liberal Thought.* Chicago: University of Chicago Press.

Meranze, Michael. 1996. *Laboratories of Virtue: Punishment, Revolution, and Authority in Philadelphia, 1760–1835.* Chapel Hill: University of North Carolina Press.

Merriam, Charles E. 1972. *History of the Theory of Sovereignty since Rousseau.* New York: Garland.

Mink, Gwendolyn. 1998. *Welfare's End.* Ithaca: Cornell University Press.

Mitchell, Stephen, trans. 1992. *The Book of Job.* New York: Harper Perennial.

Montesquieu, Baron de. 1949. *The Spirit of the Laws.* Trans. Thomas Nugent. New York: Hafner Press.

More, Thomas. 2001. *Utopia.* Trans. Clarence H. Miller. New Haven: Yale University Press.

Morris, Herbert. 1968. "Persons and Punishment." *Monist* 52, no. 4: 475–501.

Munger, Frank. 2002. "Dependency by Law: Welfare and Identity in the Lives of Poor Women." In *Lives in the Law,* ed. Austin Sarat, Lawrence Douglas, and Martha Merrill Umphrey, 83–121. Ann Arbor: University of Michigan Press.

Neumeyer, Peter. 1971. "Franz Kafka, Sugar Baron." *Modern Fiction Studies* 17, no. 1: 5–16.

New York Times. 2003. Editorial. "Two Million and Counting." May 19.

Nietzsche, Friedrich. 1989. *On the Genealogy of Morals.* Trans. Walter Kaufman and R. J. Hollingdale. New York: Vintage Books.

Nino, C. S. 1983. "A Consensual Theory of Punishment." *Philosophy and Public Affairs* 12:289–306.

Nonet, Philippe. 1995. "Sanction." *Cumberland Law Review* 25, no. 3: 489–532.

Northey, Anthony D. 1986. "Kafka and Foreign Lands: The Life Stories of His Uncles." *Journal of the Kafka Society of America* 10, no. 1–2: 68–79.

Nozick, Robert. 1974. *Anarchy, State, and Utopia.* New York: Basic Books.

Oakeshott, Michael. 1946. Introduction. In Thomas Hobbes, *Leviathan,* ed. Michael Oakershott. Oxford: Basil Blackwell.

Paine, Thomas. Laws of The Society for Political Enquiries. In American Philosophical Society archives.

———. [1791] 1995. *The Rights of Man; Common Sense; And Other Political Writings.* New York: Oxford University Press.

Parenti, Christian. 1996. "Making Prison Pay." *Nation* 262:4.

———. 1999. *Lockdown America: Police and Prisons in the Age of Crisis.* New York: Verso.

Pateman, Carol. 1988. *The Sexual Contract.* Stanford: Stanford University Press.

Peters, Paul. 2001. "Witness to the Execution: Kafka and Colonialism." *Monatshefte* 93, no. 4: 401–25.

Philadelphia Prison System Fiscal Year Report. 2001.

Piper, Karen. 1996. "The Language of the Machine: A Postcolonial Reading of Kafka." *Journal of the Kafka Society of America* 20, no. 1–2: 42–54.

"Pitt Government's Plan for Botany Bay Settlement." 1786. August 18. http://www.le.ac.uk/esh/ca26/eh400/sources.

Pitts, Jennifer. 2005. *The Turn to Empire.* Princeton: Princeton University Press.

Politzer, Heinz. 1966. *Franz Kafka: Parable and Paradox.* Ithaca: Cornell University Press.

Prison Industry Reform Legislation. 1998. Congressional Hearing. June 25.

Quinn, Warren. 1985. "The Right to Threaten and the Right to Punish." *Philosophy and Public Affairs* 14, no. 4: 327–73.

Reynolds, Morgan. 1997. "The Economic Impact of Prison Labor." National Center for Policy Analysis.

Reynolds, Morgan, and Knut Rostad. 2001. "Creating Factories behind Bars." National Center for Policy Analysis.

Robin, Corey. 2004. *Fear: The History of a Political Idea.* Oxford: Oxford University Press.

Ross, W. D. 1965. *The Right and the Good.* 56–64. Oxford: Clarendon.

Rousseau, Jean Jacques. 1968. *The Social Contract.* Trans. Maurice Cranstom. London: Penguin.

Rusche, Georg, and Otto Kirschheimer. 1939. *Punishment and Social Structure.* New York: Columbia University Press.

Rush, Benjamin. 1787. "An Inquiry into the Effects of Public Punishments upon Criminals and Society." Delivered at Society for Political Enquiries.

Sarat, Austin. 2001. "Killing Me Softly: Capital Punishment and the Technologies for Taking Life." In *Pain, Death, and the Law,* ed. Austin Sarat. Ann Arbor: University of Michigan Press.

Sassen, Saskia. 1998. *Globalization and Its Discontents.* New York: Free Press.

Schmitt, Carl. 1985. *Political Theology: Four Chapters on the Concept of Sovereignty.* Trans. George Schwab. Cambridge: MIT Press.

Schofield, Philip. 1999. "Political and Religious Radicalism in the Thought of Jeremy Bentham." *History of Political Thought* 20, no. 2: 272–91.

Shklar, Judith. 1991. *American Citizenship: The Quest for Inclusion.* Cambridge: Harvard University Press.

———. 1998. "The Political Theory of Utopia: From Melancholy to Nostalgia." In *Political Thought and Political Thinkers,* ed. Stanley Hoffman. Chicago: University of Chicago Press.

Simon, Jonathan. 1993. *Poor Discipline.* Chicago: University of Chicago Press.

———. 1997. "Governing through Crime in a Democratic Society" Paper presented at American Sociological Association Meeting, Toronto.

Simon, Jonathan, and Malcolm Feeley. 1995. "True Crime: The New Penology and the Public Discourse on Crime." In *Punishment and Social Control*, ed. T. Blomberg and S. Cohen. New York: Aldine de Gruyter.

Skinner, Quentin. 1978. *The Foundation of Modern Political Thought*. Cambridge: Cambridge University Press.

Smith, A. E. 2000. *Colonists in Bondage: White Servitude and Convict Labour in America, 1607–1776*. Baltimore: Clearfield Company.

Steinberg, Erwin R. 1976. "The Judgment in Kafka's 'In the Penal Colony.'" *Journal of Modern Literature* 5, no. 3.

Steves, David. 2001. "As Many Oregonians Lose Work, Prisons Add Inmate Jobs." *Register Guard*, December 24.

Taylor, A. E. 1965. "The Ethical Doctrine of Hobbes." In *Hobbes; Studies, by Leo Strauss [and others]*, ed. K. Brown, 35–56. Cambridge, MA: Harvard University Press.

Teeters, Negley K. 1955. *The Cradle of the Penitentiary: The Walnut Street Jail at Philadelphia, 1793–1835*. Publication sponsored by Pennsylvania Prison Society.

Thoreau, Henry David. 1997. "Civil Disobedience." In *Political Thought in the United States: A Documentary History*, ed. Lynn Tower Sargent. New York: New York University Press.

Tocqueville, Alexis de. 1969. *Democracy in America*. Ed. J. P. Mayer. New York: Harper and Row.

Tocqueville, Alexis de, and Gustave de Beaumont. 1970. *The Penitentiary System in the United States and Its Application in France*. New York: Augustus Kelley.

Toth, Stephen A. 1999. "Colonisation or Incarceration?" *Journal of Pacific History* 34, no. 1: 59–74.

Transportation Statute. 1717. *Statues at Large, from Magna Charta to 1761*, carefully collated and revised by Danby Pickering. Vol. 5. Cambridge, 1762.

Tuck, Richard. 1993. *Philosophy and Government, 1572–1651*. Cambridge: Cambridge University Press.

Tully, James. 1990. "Political Freedom." *Journal of Philosophy* 87:517–23.

Turnbull, Robert J. 1796. "A Visit to the Philadelphia Prison." Philadelphia: Budd and Betram. American Philosophical Society Library.

Uggen, Christopher, and Jeff Manza. 2002. "Democratic Contraction? Political Consequences of Felon Disenfranchisement in the United States." *American Sociological Review* 67: 777–803.

United Nations, Economic and Social Council. 2006. Commission on Human Rights. "Situation of Detainees at Guantanamo Bay." Report released February 15.

Warrender, Howard. 1957. *The Political Philosophy of Hobbes: His Theory of Obligation*. Oxford: Oxford University Press.

Weber, Max. 1948. "Politics as a Vocation." In *From Max Weber: Essays in Sociology*. New York: Taylor and Francis.

Weil, Simone. 1987. *The Need for Roots: Prelude to a Declaration of Duties towards Mankind*. Trans. A. F. Wills. London: Routledge and Kegan Paul.

Weinstein, Arnold. 1990. "Kafka's Writing Machine: Metamorphosis in the Penal Colony." In *Critical Essays on Franz Kafka*, ed. Ruth V. Gross, 120–49. Boston: G. K. Hall.

Western, Bruce. 2006. *Punishment and Inequality*. New York: Russell Sage Foundation.

Western, Bruce, and Katherine Beckett. 1999. "How Unregulated Is the U.S. Labor Market? The Penal System as a Labor Market Institution." *American Journal of Sociology* 104, no. 4: 1030–60.

White, Thomas I. "The Key to Nowhere: Pride and Utopia." In *Interpreting Thomas More's "Utopia,"* ed. John C. Olin, 37–60. New York: Fordham University Press.

Index